PRAISE FOR INHERIT

I have known Lisa and Lorena for more than twenty years and have admired their work in serving vulnerable children and families. We can all benefit from knowing the experiences and underlying values that have shaped their lives. I look forward to sharing this inheritance with my children and grandchildren.
Hope Andrade, Texas Secretary of State

Dr. Gonzalez has been a member of the USHLI family for years, sharing her leadership and cultural expertise with hundreds of high school and college students annually. Grounded in *Familia*, she enables students to see their past challenges and triumphs as valuable examples of ways to bring about social, economic, and political change. Dr. Gonzalez helps us all recognize that our Latino experience is an invaluable inheritance that should be cultivated and shared with future generations of Latino leaders.
Dr. Juan Andrade, US Hispanic Leadership Institute

More than ever, we need to take the best from our past to move us into the future. Through this collection of stories, Dr. Gonzalez has highlighted those values we need to carry our country forward. From welcoming the stranger, to serving the marginalized—let's discover the best of our cultural inheritance and teach it to our children and their children.
Henry Cisneros, Executive Chairman, CityView

One of the most important contributions that our nation's growing Latino community can offer to all of us who have benefited from growing up with the values of family, hard work, and sacrifice, is to amplify these ideals for our journey into a more diverse American future. These stories remind us of the values that make us strong as individuals, families, and communities.
Noel Costellanos, President, Christian Community Development Association

There is no greater call than to serve with a Servant Heart, and Lorena embodies this spirit completely. We have worked together for over fifteen years with our gente, bridging our past values and experiences to our present hopes and dreams. These stories are an extension of the authors' work with our Latino community, bringing healing, peace, laughter, and the affirmation that we are all leaders!
Consuelo Castillo Kickbusch, President, Educational Achievement Services Inc.

Having known much about Lisa Treviño Cummins' family (personally or told to me by others) there is much to share. [These] stories will make a great contribution, not only for today, but for those that are coming behind us.
Dr. Jesse Miranda, Chief Executive Director, National Hispanic Christian Leadership Council

Through the National Hispana Leadership Institute, I had the distinct honor of engaging with Dr. Lorena Gonzalez who then introduced me to another remarkable Latina leader, Lisa Cummins. I've experienced firsthand their passion to provide loving care and service to "the people" in the course of their work. Their commitment and leadership unleashes the potential for so much more to come. Expect it!

Marieli E. Colon Padilla, Board Chair, National Hispana Leadership Institute

INHERITANCE

Discovering the Richness of Latino Family & Culture

by
Lorena Garza Gonzalez
with
Lisa Treviño Cummins

ISBN: 978-0615668772

Urban Strategies
Arlington, Virginia

Printed in the United States of America

Cover design by Sarah Ondrey Johnson
Photos provided by Gabrielle Polanco and the Garza
Gonzalez and Treviño Cummins Families

This book is dedicated to the thousands of unique and diverse families who have provided unforgettable examples and lessons in my twenty-year career of serving Latino families. Through them, my life's purpose has been revealed and my work has been defined with meaning and joy, even in the midst of heartache. Members of my own *familia,* both in Mexico and in the United States, have been key actors in this, *mi vida hermosa.* Starring in these roles have been my husband, Rene; and my children, Rene, Evan, and Amanda. Additionally, my parents, Homer and Maria (Choco) Garza, and my brother, Arnol; his wife, Monica; and their children, Nicholas and Michael. I truly am blessed and thank God every day for His many gifts. Without His constant presence, my *familia* would be incomplete.—*Lorena G. Gonzalez*

I dedicate this book to my husband, Wayne, for embracing and celebrating my Hispanic heritage as if it were his own. And to Rachel, Jonathan, and David for your love and support. You guys are *awesome.* What a privilege I have to be your mom! *xoxoxo.* To my parents who modeled for me the generosity, courage, and resourcefulness that I hope to emulate. To my three brothers—you are the best! And to my grandparents, who showed me what it means to live faithfully and with laughter, even in the most difficult of circumstances. More than any, I thank my Lord for His love, grace, and mercy. He has been faithful even when I was without faith. He has loved me even when I didn't deserve it. And He has inspired me to love the widow, orphan, and vulnerable.—*Lisa Treviño Cummins*

CONTENTS

INTRODUCTION   2

MI CASA ES SU CASA   5

PROMISING THE WORLD   11

"SUPER DELUXE" CREATIVITY   19

HOME AWAY FROM HOME   25

THE GIFT OF MUSIC   31

HOMEGROWN LEADERSHIP   37

LAS COLONIAS   43

LA LIBERTAD   53

LOOKING BEYOND OUR PAST   59

DEVOTION   67

LA LOCA AND THE SNEETCHES   75

SHARED FAMILY DREAMS   81

WOMEN AHEAD OF THEIR TIME   85

GUATEMALAN ANGEL   95

THE FAMILY WE CHOOSE   101

MR. JEWELRY   107

THE MEXICAN POWER NAP   113

THE WOMAN IN THE
    "NO-ONE-WILL-SEE-ME" OUTFIT   119
RESPETO MISUNDERSTOOD   127
NADA SE LE COMPLICA   133
HONORING EL TRABAJADOR   139
TRADITION   145
LIVING FAITH   151
JUMPING THE FENCE   157
LA BENDICIÓN   161
OUR BENDICIÓN   165

ACKNOWLEDGMENTS   166
BIOGRAPHIES   168
PHOTO ALBUM   170

INHERITANCE

INTRODUCTION

Recently, I had the opportunity to enjoy dinner in a very exclusive restaurant in Las Vegas with a group of accomplished business people. We talked about friends and families, among many other topics, but throughout the evening it was quite clear that our definition of "success" was different—theirs somewhat focused on portfolios and future earning potential, and mine on social change. Don't get me wrong, I enjoy earning what I'm worth and securing a comfortable quality of life, but money has never been a driving force for me.

As we talked at dinner, I heard several exchanges about "inheritance." Some viewed their retirement as the inheritance that would be left to their children, while others spoke about the inheritance they had been left by their families. "My father was in oil and left a nice nest egg," one person said. "I've inherited a beautiful historic home," another added.

I sat thinking about my own inheritance. Pop, as I lovingly called my father, came to the United States to work in the spinach fields, and later he became a cook and a welder. Pop never achieved significant financial wealth, but I've always viewed my life as abundantly rich.

It occurred to me, as I sat listening that evening, that mine is a very different kind of inheritance. My inheritance comes in the form of family and love. What I have inherited is a strong faith, a will to persevere, a desire to be inclusive, the honor of hard work, and the beauty of my culture. It's an inheritance money can't buy. It's priceless. My Latino inheritance guides me every day of my life. It's made me who I am. It brings me hope and peace.——*LGG*

As you read this collection of stories, we hope you will celebrate the best of our culture and values, discover the jewels of your own stories, and pass forward the blessings of our inheritance.

Our inheritance comes to us in various ways. Some are God-given genetics, where we don't have a choice of what we inherit. Some things we have the opportunity to inherit but don't want to do so because they are hurtful. But there are many gifts of inheritance we can pass on to our children that are determined by our choice. What is it that we will give our children? Will we share with them a heart of thankfulness for our many blessings? Will we share with them the ability to see the "diamonds in the rough" that comes through difficulty and heartache? This collection of stories includes the many ideas, experiences, traditions, and values that I want to be sure I pass on to my children—the most important being around the ideas of loving God wholeheartedly and loving others well.——LTC

Mi Casa Es Su Casa

Our family was accustomed to unexpected and unknown visitors, urgent phone calls from a family member in Mexico, or trips in the middle of the night to help someone in our community. Somehow among Latinos, we think we are all related, *primo de uno, comadre del otro*/cousin of one, buddy of the other. Even a weak link is link enough to warrant help.

The day Cheto arrived was no different from any other. My mother had prepared a delicious dinner of *caldo de res*—a meal that infused our home with the smell of beef, cilantro, carrots, potatoes, and corn tortillas. Just before dinner, I was asked to cut the *limones* for the *caldo*, because a *caldo* without lemon or limes is, well, not *caldo*! As I was cutting *limones*, I heard the doorbell ring. Since she was busy tending to our dinner, my mother yelled through the halls of the house, *"Contestén"*/"Answer the door." But my father didn't seem to hear her as Lucha Villa and Los Panchos played in the background, accompanied by an occasional *"Ajúa."*

Realizing no one had responded to the bell, we all moved toward the door at the same time to find a small gentleman with a brilliant smile and a head full of bright red hair. He stretched out his arms and exclaimed, "Soy Cheto!"

We froze and stared at this man, who kept enthusiastically jumping up and down to proclaim his arrival. I heard my dad ask under his breath, *"¿Pues, quien es hombre?"*/"Who is this man?" My mother answered, *"No se"*/"I don't know," equally quiet so she would not offend Cheto.

At this point, I wanted to shut the door and get on with the *caldo* that was awaiting us. But not my parents. My mother asked, "Cheto?" He replied, *"Soy Cheto, hermano de tu cuñada de la cuidad de Penjamo"*/"I'm Cheto, the brother of your sister-in-law from the city of Penjamo." I was puzzled. Where was Penjamo? My parents began to crack a forced smile, but not with the same level of enthusiasm that came from Cheto. *"Soy el hermano de Coco,"* he exclaimed. My parents began to nod their heads, now willingly, and smiled—the confirmation of blood line seemed to be affirmed. Coco, it turned out, was my dad's brother's wife, and Cheto was her brother. Although we had never met Cheto, he came from Penjamo, Mexico, and that was enough.

Culture has a way of connecting us. We were now Cheto's family, and welcoming him was a way of repaying all those families who helped my dad when he arrived in the United States.

The interactions I witnessed as Cheto became a part of our home for a short time became the backbone of my definition of family—individuals connected by culture, struggles, dreams, hope, and sometimes even a weak blood link. This would not be the last time we would share this form of hospitality. Throughout my life, I recall many uncles who came through our home while they found work and settled in for a long, or short-term, stay. Often we were the first step of a long journey for newly arrived families, part of a network that supported this move to the country of opportunity.
—LGG

Our Latino culture enjoys the common gift of hospitality. I remember growing up with so many different individuals who, at my parents' invitation, found refuge when they had no other place to lay their head. Among them I remember a Mexican immigrant who, with her infant son, had no place to call home. There was the woman whose husband was abusive, the teenager who was having trouble at home, and the young man who was moving from another state to make a new life for himself.

In our country's history, we have welcomed families who were attempting to pursue a better life through settlement houses. In our Latino community culture, the settlement houses were our very own homes—living out that traditional Spanish saying of *"Mi casa es su casa,"/"My home is your home."*—LTC

PROMISING THE WORLD

I was asked some years ago to help a production crew obtain footage of families living in challenging conditions. I asked a sweet family I knew if they would be interested. This small family, led by Pedro and his wife, Mini, was excited and proud to be the focus of a television interview. Energized by their enthusiasm, I called the production team to give them Pedro's address and arrange a time to meet. There was an uncomfortable silence on the phone, and I realized the crew leader was fearful of going to the barrio on Saltillo Street where Pedro and Mini lived. For a moment I was stunned and angry. Wasn't he the one who asked me to find a family living in a challenging situation? Did he know the beauty of the neighborhood's cultural arts, the colorful murals, and the history of our faith and traditions? Presidents and the Pope had even made time to come to the community surrounding Saltillo Street. I swallowed my anger and assured him he would be safe visiting Pedro and Mini.

We arrived at Pedro and Mini's home in broad day-light at two in the afternoon. Even though I was certain my *compañeros*/partners would feel safe, they arrived at Pedro's in a big white van with their faces filled with apprehension. Slowly, reluctantly, they began to unload their lights, cameras, screen reflectors, and other equipment.

Pedro's bright pink, wood-framed house was a bit lop-sided and in need of many structural repairs. Toys filled the front yard along with a barbecue pit for making *carne asada*/grilled steak. As we entered the modest home, I quickly realized the immense pride Pedro felt as he welcomed us. *"Bienvenidos"*/"Welcome to our home," he said. I couldn't read the expressions on the faces of the cameramen, because they were behind me, but I wondered if they were feeling pity, disgust, or fear. Nonetheless, we entered.

In addition to the living room, this small house had a kitchen, one bedroom, and one bathroom. Pedro made a practice of decorating his home with his children's art, which was really a display of his pride in his children. In addition, homemade toys and modestly framed family photographs made their home feel warm and inviting. On a light fixture, in the middle of the room, hung a large plastic beach ball, emblazoned with a map of the world. I thought it looked charming, but wasn't sure why it was located so prominently in the room.

As the cameramen sat on a couch, Pedro immediately jumped up. *"Que mal educado"*/"I have bad manners,

I didn't offer you anything to drink." The two gentle-men immediately declined. "No! I mean, no, thanks," one said. "I'd like some," I followed up. "It's warm outside and some water would be great." Pedro told me he had only lemon-flavored Kool-Aid. "That's my favorite," I assured him.

The crew continued to set up and attempted to avoid stepping on the little girl who crawled around them, playing with her books and beautiful homemade toys. I could hear mumblings between the two cameramen, but I couldn't make out what they were saying. By the expression on their faces, they seemed uncomfortable and a bit angry.

As they were making last-minute adjustments to the lighting and the angle of the camera, the two men were concerned about the beach ball dangling from the light fixture. "Who would hang a world globe beach ball in the middle of their living room?" one snickered to the other. I began to feel uncomfortable. We were in Pedro's home, and to disrespect him was a violation of how I had been raised. "Let's just try and get a shot without the ball and start the interview," the other cameraman said.

I explained to Pedro and his family how the process would move forward and the type of questions I would ask. "It's a bit scary," Mini said. Indeed it was. Their modest living room had been invaded by unfamiliar faces, equipment, and lighting.

As Pedro began to answer my first question, I saw the cameraman roll his eyes in frustration because the beach ball was in the middle of his shot. In spite of his efforts to tap it away from the camera, the ball swung back to the middle of the frame. Finally, after several sighs of frustration and continued attempts to tap the hanging ball out of the camera's view, the cameraman complained, "This ridiculous ball is in the way!"

I cringed with embarrassment and tried to remedy the tense situation. *"Oye,* Pedro, the camera guys are having a hard time capturing your beautiful family because the globe beach ball is in the shot. Is there any way we can take it down?" I asked. The two cameramen stood silently. Pedro stood up and hugged his ten-month-old daughter tightly. She was bright-eyed with a smile that communicated joy and happiness. *"Miré"*/"Look," he said, "I am poor and have no college education. I work two jobs for my family. I love my wife and my daughter so much. I know I am not much, but one day I plan to have much. You see, I promised my family the world, and right now this is all I can give them—this silly beach ball with the world on it. So if it's okay with you, I would like to keep it up."

I turned to the cameramen, and with tears in his eyes, one said, "He wants the same thing for his daughter that I want for mine." Quickly the equipment was set to be certain the beach ball hung prominently in the shot.

When the interview was finished and all the equipment had been returned to the van, I watched as each crew member gave Pedro and Mini a heartfelt *abrazo/* hug. Their worlds, and mine, had been changed forever.——*LGG*

More often than we realize, many of us misinterpret the motivations of others because we see them through lenses shaped by our own culture and experiences. Sometimes these lenses can serve as protective factors, preventing us from harm. These lenses, however, can also hinder us from those things that can give life, like relationships and community. Just as Mini and Pedro were initially looked down upon for what others deemed silly, the marginalized are often misunderstood when, in fact, their hopes, dreams, and aspirations are common to most.

In one of many situations where I have recognized my own lens of culture, experience, and values, I was introduced to research focused on why so many low-income women choose to have babies before getting married. Putting the moral and ethical issues aside, the fact is that unwed mothers set their children up for a life of poverty. While there are certainly exceptions, the data shows this result to be the general rule.

Before I read the study, I attributed single mothers having babies to, among other things, individual irresponsibility and immaturity. And while irresponsibility and immaturity may be part of the explanation, for some, the issues are more complex. The vast majority of the women participating in this unprecedented research highlighted two things that surprised me and prompted me to understand low-income single mothers in a different way.

The first revelation was learning that women in the study were so desirous to be loved unconditionally, they had babies they hoped would grow up to be children who would love their mothers wholeheartedly, no matter the circumstances. Since the women had seen and experienced so many broken relationships, they believed that the children they bore would never abandon them and, as a result, would provide them with the forever kind of love they longed for.

Secondly, the study revealed that many low-income women have such a high regard for marriage, they are afraid they will tarnish this institution they idealize. Admirably, they didn't want to take the risk of "messing marriage up," reflecting their value for marriage but perhaps without the tools, skills, and knowledge on how to develop healthy relationships and marriages.

Whether it is mistaking a mother's pursuit for love as she raises children alone or not recognizing that simple things like a beach ball reflect deep aspirations, the different lenses we wear can cause us to miss the *beauty in others. The challenge is to recognize these lenses and to see past them to find our shared hopes, discover the dignity of all, and recognize we have all been divinely created for a divine purpose.—LTC*

"Super Deluxe" Creativity

It was the first day in middle school and we had just moved into a new neighborhood with a larger house but a smaller circle of friends. The people in my old neighborhood were my cousins, and my new neighbors were very different from me. Most kids in the new neighborhood had blue eyes and spoke only English, and the girls had shiny, long, sun-goddess blond hair. I, on the other hand, had Aztec Indian princess hair—jet black, long, and straight.

I was dressed in a hipster '70s-style outfit that first day of school. I wanted to be cool and fit in, but within five minutes I realized I was different. It was their hair and their amazing, bouncy curls that set us apart. I didn't want to change my hair color, but I instantly knew I needed curls!

One girl stood out above all others. I was determined to find out how she created the mane of curls that exploded on her head. "How did you get your hair so curly?" I casually asked. She explained that she used something new called *"Electric Curlers."* She said the words very slowly and in a loud voice as if I came from a foreign planet and couldn't understand. "Wow," I said, "where did you get the *'Electric Curlers?'"* She told me she bought them at Kmart. "How much did they cost?" Not knowing the value of money, I acknowledged the price she told me and went on with my school business. But I couldn't quit thinking about *"Electric Curlers."*

After school my mom met me at the door and asked, "So, *mija*, what did you learn today in school?" I didn't tell her anything about math or history—which is what she expected to hear. I told her about the beautiful, curly hair I had seen at school. "Ma, all the girls at school have their *pelo todo chinito"/*"hair all curly."

"Si, mija, ¿como le hacen?"/"How do they do it?" she asked.

"Pues, Ma, es algo que se llama 'electric curlers'"/ "Well, Mom, it's something they call *'Electric Curlers.'"*

My mother's eyes widened, and she slowly repeated, "Electric curlers?" I then told her they were purchased from Kmart and cost $60. The blood rose in my mother's cheeks.

"¿Que, que, SIXTY dolares?"/"What, sixty dollars?" "Yes," I said meekly.

She quickly responded that this was equivalent to a month's worth of groceries. I thought for a moment—eat for a month or have curly hair? I knew deep down that my hair would remain straight.

That night I sat with my family in our "multipurpose room" (the dining, family, and living room along with my brother's bedroom) watching a high-drama novela. I couldn't concentrate on the novela because I kept wondering how I would get the curls so I could fit into my new school. What a dilemma.

I was on the floor against my mother's knees as she sat on the bed watching the novela. All of a sudden she began to work with my hair, pulling it so tightly I thought I would lose my breath. At first I thought she was angry at me for having the audacity to ask for $60, but then she rolled a section of my hair around one of my brother's socks and tied the two ends in a knot! She took another section of my hair, and then another, until my entire head was covered in socks!

"*¿Ma, que haces?*"/"Mom, what have you done?" I asked.

"You wanted curly hair, you will have curly hair," my mother responded in her best English. But these were not Kmart electric curlers, I thought to myself. This was a half-baked solution that I was sure would result in a bad, Orphan Annie look.

The next morning could not come fast enough. I woke up early to have plenty of time to straighten my hair if the sock method didn't work out. But as I untied each one of the socks and removed them from my head, a perfect curl formed. When I was all done, I stood before the mirror and looked at the most amazing head of curls I had ever seen—better than the stars of the novelas, better than any models on the cover of the *Vanidades* or *Glamour* magazines, and better than any of the curls of my new classmates!

I walked into school with an extra bounce in my step to announce my new hairstyle. The beautiful blond girl was the first to come up to me and exclaim, "Your hair looks fabulous! Did you get the electric curlers?" I stood tall and proud and with gusto I said, "Yes, I did!" She asked if I'd purchased the Super Deluxe model. I shook my curly head and neither confirmed nor denied the innovative "model" my mother had created. It really was super deluxe. With a handful of socks my mother made certain her daughter felt secure and happy at her new school.—*LGG*

It's been said that necessity is the mother of invention. We don't know the impetus for Hispanic inventions like the color television or the discovery of sugar nucleotides and their role in the biosynthesis of carbohydrates (for which the inventor won the Nobel Peace

Prize)—but you, dear reader, now know the story that precipitated the soon-to-be-famous sock-curling technique.

Perhaps because of the absence of privilege and the difficulty in accessing resources, many in our Hispanic community must rely on being resourceful and entrepreneurial. I remember as a child that my grandparents would dry the gourds that were cut off from vines they had grown and use them for all sorts of cleaning purposes. The gourds, or estropajos, were dried in the kitchen, on the clothesline, or on the fence in the hot sun. As a young adult, I then saw that dried gourds were being marketed by major retailers and boutiques as newly discovered "earth friendly," all-natural loofah pads.

These characteristics of innovation and resourcefulness were also evident in my parents, who in spite of their limited resources, started a small machine shop that eventually outgrew our home garage and employed twenty individuals. My uncles also launched a chain of hair salons that provided employment opportunities for two generations of cousins and more. Whether it is sock curlers or machining lathes, we can learn from those whose desire for a better life motivated them to work hard, take risks, and be creative. Who knows what new discoveries will be made as we pass these values of entrepreneurialism and resourcefulness on to the next generation.——LTC

HOME AWAY FROM HOME

Growing up with immigrant parents who had one foot in Mexico and the other in the United States, I became accustomed to frequent border-crossing travel. Like clockwork, our summer and winter holidays entailed countless hours by car, bus, and/or train. And we never traveled alone but in packs, with a high-spirited company of cousins, aunts, uncles, and a few others I didn't exactly know.

In the winter, we rushed our trip between school breaks and my father's work schedule, so we would not miss the Mexican Christmas traditions that included *posadas* and *tamale* making, and a host of activities for the New Year celebration.

As for the summer, our trip began immediately on the last day of school. When the bell rang for dismissal, my dad would pick us up at the school campus in a truck loaded with boxes containing clothes and other items to give to our family in Mexico. I dreaded that pickup, as it looked as if I was joining a caravan with all the trappings of a gypsy life boxed in the truck. Although every other Mexican family did the same, I was still embarrassed.

Because of his work schedule, my father was able to join us for only two weeks of our summer vacation. So, he would drop us off at the Los Angeles train station, where we boarded for a two-day trip to Del Rio, Texas. Being on the train meant we would alternate between sitting in a seat for long periods of time, and running up and down the aisles until my mother would call us back for tacos and empanadas she had packed to minimize our travel costs. Sometimes we would be treated to a meal in the train's dining room, where we shared sodas, french fries, and sandwiches. To make sure we split the food evenly, I gave my brother one french fry at a time. Soda proved a bit more challenging to distribute as I couldn't be sure that his gulp wasn't bigger than mine. Our mutually agreed-upon solution was to dip each french fry in the soda. By the end of our meal, greasy fat would float on the top of our cup. "Hey, it all goes down mixed up anyway," I assured my brother. "OK," he would sweetly respond. Unappetizing, yes, but equal.

After our second day on the train, we finally arrived in Del Rio, where we were met by family, who would then take us the remaining five hours to Nueva Rosita, Coahuila, Mexico. Anticipating lots of clothing boxes, we were picked up in a truck. The funny thing is that it wasn't just a truck and driver that showed up; we were also welcomed by two uncles and two *primos/*

cousins—who came along on the ride. So with about five giant boxes, my mother, brother, cousin, and I joined the five people from Mexico in the pickup truck. We were a sight to see. Many times I wondered why all these people would come for us. Didn't they know space was limited? Couldn't they wait to see us in Rosita? I am sure that if forty more cousins, aunts, and uncles could have joined, they too would have met us on our arrival in Del Rio. This desire to be together was truly reflective of our Latino culture.

As we traveled to our final destination, I'll never forget looking up in the sky to see the stars shine with a vibrancy that I've only seen in the Mexican desert. I always felt happy to be with my *primos*, to be going home to my other world, and to be secure under the sparkle of the stars. Arriving just before dawn, we soon witnessed the brilliant sunrise, as if it said *bienvenidos*/welcome to your home, Mexico!

For me there was always an adjustment period. "OK, Lorena," I would tell myself, "shift languages. Be a 'real' Mexican and blend in." Although my parents always spoke Spanish and raised us in a very traditional Mexican home, I was an American. In addition to loving Juan Miguel music, I also liked the Monkees and the Beatles.

But family trumped it all. *"Primita, te estrañamos mucho. Platicanos, ¿como son los Estados Unidos?"*/ "We miss you a lot, little cousin. Tell us what the United States is like." With wonder, my cousins would listen as I told them about our lifestyle, highlighting the television—four channels, three in English and one in Spanish. This was a big deal! If my cousins had a television, they were accustomed to only one channel that had limited viewing hours and required an antenna facing north or sometimes west, and was often covered in foil.

I've thought many times of those glittering stars of the Mexican desert and those blessed moments in the back of my uncle's pickup truck, encompassed by the feeling of pure innocence and the joy of family love.—— *LGG*

I didn't have the same type of dual citizenship experience that Lorena has had, as I am a third-generation Mexican American, but I do know what it means to be in those special places where you feel that you belong—places that feel like home. Home is more than bricks and mortar. It is a place of safety, comfort, peace, and joy. My parents made a wonderful home for my siblings and me, but they also served as the second home for many others. As a teen, the kids from our youth group would come over to hang out. It wasn't uncommon for me to call home and ask if I could bring friends home from church and, fifteen minutes later, arrive on the doorstep with twenty of my friends ready to watch a football game and eat pizza with my parents joining in the fun.

With an increasing number of us living miles away from our families, or living in homes that allow little interaction with neighbors, it is important that we are intentional in creating opportunities to engage with one another. Whether it is Sunday meals with family and friends, or taking the time to meet with neighbors, we have the opportunity to provide a sense of "home" for our community to enjoy.—LTC

The Gift of Music

All Latino gatherings are sure to find friends, family, great food, and of course, music. Music expresses both the joy and sadness of our lives—past, present, and future. Singing was a constant in our family, sometimes with a guitar but most often a cappella. When I hear songs like Jose Alfredo Jimenez's *"Solamente la Mano de Dios."* I remember the music filling my soul with raw emotion, reminding me how music allowed us the freedom to express deep feelings. With music, we were able to forget the circumstances of the day and hope for a better future.

The summer soundtrack of my visits to Mexico was created from the music I heard in my Tio Chuy's house, which was next door to my grandmother. All of Tio Chuy's seven children were blessed with beautiful voices. They could belt out a note at any moment—and they did, all day long. Most mornings you didn't need an alarm clock because *"Las Canteras"/*"The Singers" sung loud enough for all of the neighborhood to hear.

Some days, the songs that came from my uncle's house were filled with lost love. Other times, the singing soothed tragic moments. I loved music so much that I dreamed of becoming a performer, dancing and singing to sold-out audiences around the world. There was only one problem—I couldn't carry a tune.

One summer morning, with a heart desirous of filling the air with a song to express my own passion, I went to Tio Chuy's via our normal entry point (the kitchen window). Feeling safe and confident by the familiar aroma of homemade tortillas, *chorizo*, and brewing coffee, I stood in Tio Chuy's living room and belted out a song. As if a sleeping giant was released, I was *singing!* This was so completely unplanned and spontaneous that I even marveled at what I was doing. At the shock of this "joyful noise," my cousins stopped talking and looked straight at me. I waited for their laughter and teasing, but instead, they smiled and said, *"Te avientas para cantar, prima"/*"You sang great, cousin!" Although most people would have dismissed my effort, I was loved and made part of *"Las Canteras."* They understood that music and singing from the heart, regardless of the quality, was precious.

Today I'm still moved as I hear my father and my eldest son, arm-in-arm, singing old songs in unison. Often they throw out a *grito,* with tears running down their cheeks. I can't carry a tune, but I learned something very important during my summers in Mexi-

co—in spite of circumstances, music can make our lives richer. Music is a gift to be treasured and shared.
—*LGG*

Music played as large a role in my family as it did in Lorena's. My maternal grandfather, six of his eight children, and many grandchildren are either musicians or singers. My father has carried the tradition of music from his mother to our immediate family.

When my parents host family and friends in their home, the real party begins when Dad takes out the guitar and starts playing some of the old musical favorites, ranging from the romantic "Sabor A Mi" to the gospel songs we sang as children. Regardless of whether we're together or apart, birthdays are not complete without my father playing "Happy Birthday" on the guitar with my mom joining in the singing.

Dad hasn't given up on trying to develop his own bee-bopping family singing group. The pattern is always the same. Dad gets us started with a warm-up "do-re-me-fa-so-la-ti-do." That's when the laughing begins. Then he tries to get us to sing "Ahhhh," in four-part harmony. That's when the hysterical laughing begins. He then flows into his B. B. King version of "On Blueberry Hill" where we all try to sing along. The hysterical laughing continues. The music, interspersed with hysterical laughing, goes on for about an hour until we're completely exhausted. What a time we have together hosting our in-house family concert and musical comedy!—LTC

HOMEGROWN LEADERSHIP

One year just before Christmas, I was called to an emergency board meeting to approve a budget for a local social service organization. This wasn't the best timing since I already had plans to join our family at our annual *tamalada*. But because I'd made a commitment as a board member, I reluctantly attended.

Though I was frustrated and restless as the meeting went on longer than anticipated, I watched with interest how our board chair, a president and CEO of a local bank, helped board members of varying levels of expertise navigate through the reports and decisions before them. She fielded numerous questions such as, What personnel would be needed? How would they be trained? Are there necessary supplies and equipment to meet goals? How is quality control being managed to ensure that services delivered are meeting expectations? Finally, after this two-hour meeting that felt like four, I quickly headed to my mother's house, where I knew my family was waiting to begin our annual *tamalada*.

When I arrived, I smelled the aroma of *carne de puerco*/pork. My family was seated at the kitchen table, dressed in aprons and holding cooking utensils in each hand as if they were ready for battle. *"Como te tardaste, mija, ya tenemos tres horas esperandote"*/ "You took a long time, sweetheart, we've been waiting for three hours!" I apologized, grabbed the apron neatly folded on my chair, and lined up along with the others ready to work. As if calling a meeting into session, my mother sat at the head of the table and addressed the group of cousins, in-laws, and children. She first made mention of my tardiness and then quickly moved to the status of the current novela, *Siempre Te Amaré*/"I Will Always Love You." Next, she reviewed the latest *chisme*/updates, told us about an ailment of an elderly friend, and informed us it was time to commence the artful tradition of *tamale* making.

On the table were the essentials—a plastic covering for the table, spoons of every size, *hojas*/corn husks, *masa*/corn spread, and glistening in the center of the table, the soul of the traditional Mexican *tamal* . . . *la carne de puerco*/the pork meat.

My mother, an experienced *tamalera,* started by reviewing the process by which we were to spread the masa— not too much meat or the tamale would wind up too thick, she said. Mom reminded us that we had to make forty dozen. "So make the masa and meat last," she directed.

Observing that my daughter was struggling, Mom came to her side to model the technique. *"Andale, así, muy buen trabajo"*/"OK, that's how, good job," she said. And then she affirmed my friend's skill, *"Muy bien, tu si sabes"*/"Very good, you sure know how."

My mother urged us to work quickly because we were short on time. Remember she said, forty dozen and no less. *"Es lo que calcule"*/"That is what I budgeted." She assigned my nephews the task of differentiating the pork tamales from those filled with refried beans and chicken. They tore a small strip of *la hoja*/corn husk and tied one around the tamal for pork, two for beans, and three for chicken. Mom flashed a big smile of approval and pride at the work of her grandsons.

Hours later, our annual *tamalada* came to an end. The last *tamal* was wrapped and placed in a large can to be cooked to perfection. I sat reflecting on this beautiful tradition, the fun, the shared stories and dreams. But something much greater impressed me. What I witnessed in my mother that night was a leader in action, similar to the bank CEO who navigated our board meeting earlier that night. The chair of the board of directors and my mother were strategic planners. They had budgets to meet. They modeled skills, answered questions, provided positive reinforcement, and made others feel they could do this task and solve problems on their own.—*LGG*

There have been a number of studies reviewing the fact that there are not enough Latinos in elected office, on corporate boards, and in places of influence. However, this is not to say that we are without leaders. Leadership in the Latino community looks different. While we do have wonderful national leaders in individuals such as Dr. Jesse Miranda, Consuelo Kickbush, and Henry Cisneros, we also have a vast cadre of leaders whose importance is often unknown.

I think of a leader like Jose C. in Arlington, Virginia, who at times has worked two jobs so that while his children were young, they could have the benefits of a stay-at-home mother and the necessary resources for school supplies. Or Guille Sastre in Phoenix, Arizona, who in response to a need in her community, started a nonprofit organization in her home to strengthen families and now has served thousands with quality programming. Or Pastor Victor Rodriguez in San Antonio, Texas, who has been willing to break the mold of a traditional church and has taken risks to be responsive to the community's needs. None of these individuals is perfect, but they are leaders who have stepped out and taken risks with a conviction that compels them to serve others. They are just a few of the many leaders, the unsung heroes and heroines, in our country whose daily work improves our neighborhoods and country one family at a time.—LTC

LAS COLONIAS

Sections of the Rio Grande Valley are among America's most impoverished communities. Not unlike the deplorable conditions in Appalachia or the Mississippi Delta, the 400,000 residents of this destitute area have long been plagued by conditions similar to underdeveloped countries. While there have recently been some signs of improvement, these neighborhoods, or *Colonias*, have historically been characterized by unsafe housing, high unemployment, a failing educational system, and the absence of adequate drinking water and sewage systems, fueling rampant sickness.

My experience in *las Colonias* came during the heat of the summer as I worked on a research project conducting interviews with families in this area of intense poverty.

As my guide and I arrived for one 10 a.m. interview, we visited a house with a camping trailer parked outside. I began walking toward the house, but my guide redirected me and told me the family we were visiting actually lived in the camper. "Here?" I asked in shock. "This is not a house. It's a camper you hitch to the back of a car!" She offered an apologetic smile and asked that I follow her.

As we approached, I saw the camper was surrounded by plants potted in coffee cans. Pastel flowers blossomed from each can outlining the dilapidated camper. The mother greeted us at the door with a ten-month-old baby on her hip. *"Bienvenida, Dra. Gonzalez, a su casa"*/"Welcome, Dr. Gonzalez, to your house."

I walked through the door and entered a small kitchen. There I saw a hot plate with two burners that served as the stove, a small ice chest that had become the refrigerator, a larger bowl with water that was the sink, and two boxes stacked with an array of canned goods—the pantry.

I slowly turned from looking at the kitchen space to the tiny area on the other side of a curtain with a bed, a small television, a large crucifix, a picture of the Virgen de Guadalupe, and a dresser. That was the extent of the home—at most 400 square feet—where a mother and father were raising their three children.

It was all I could do to fight back tears when this woman asked us to sit on her bed to *platicar*/visit. Holding her bouncing baby in her arms, she beamed with pride as she told me of her two elementary school children who were doing well—having received all *As* and placed on the honor roll. As she spoke, her beautiful face beamed with pride.

She continued to share with me what she called *"la buena noticia"*/"good news"—she was pregnant with their fourth child, and her husband had received a small raise that would allow them to move into a home with two bedrooms. Wondering how the couple ever found a moment alone, I smiled and said it would be good that she and her husband could have privacy while their children slept in a separate room. *"O no, estamos muy acostumbrados a dormir juntos y queremos seguir unidos"*/"Oh no, we are used to sleeping together, and we want to stay united," she said. I asked where their children would have the space to do homework, read, or simply relax. *"Voy a convertir el segundo cuarto en una biblioteca"*/"I'm going to convert the second room into a library," she said. *"Quiero tiener un lugar para estudiar"*/"I want them to have a place to study."

When I asked where her bathroom was located, she told me to follow her outside behind the camper. *"Mire, mi vecina es muy buena"*/"My neighbor is so kind," she said as she pointed to a long green hose that had been dragged from the neighbor's yard and connected to a makeshift shower consisting of a six-foot basketball frame with a sheet hanging from the hoop. I was shocked, and my heart broke for her. *"Y señora, donde hacen el . . ."*/"And ma'am, where do you . . ." as I paused, somewhat embarrassed, she interrupted as she understood my unstated question. *"Mire, tenemos todo este monte para usar como baño"*/

"Look, we have all this land to use as a toilet," she responded.

As we walked back to the front yard, I was crying inside. I felt sorry for this family and mentally began working through my contacts and networks, trying to piece together a solution to help them with the basic necessities. Nobody living in this country should endure these conditions. This was not right, *pobrecitos*!

I began to offer my gratitude for her time, and I know she saw the sadness in my eyes. "Dra. Gonzalez," she said, trying to console me, *"Nosotros somos felices"*/ "We are happy." She told me they had more in the United States than they ever had in their native land. She said her family had a plan to work together to secure an education and reach their dreams. *"En este lindo país se puede hacer todo"*/"In this lovely country, one can do it all." She said her family was safe and free of violence, her children had an opportunity to get an education, and her husband was hardworking. With God, they were not discouraged by their current circumstances, *"Lo tenemos todo"*/"We have it all!"

I arrived back at my hotel and began to cry—not because of what I had seen, but because of what I failed to see. I had measured happiness in things that matter little, forgetting the things that matter most—hard work, family, and faith. This amazing woman was enjoying things that money can't buy—she taught me that I was using material goods and financial success to define my life. I left *las Colonias* more inspired than ever before. I was reminded that simplicity is not ordinary, it is extraordinary. I have never forgotten this family who helped me redefine success.——*LGG*

For years the government has attempted to intervene and turn las Colonias *around, but unfortunately, there has been limited success. In 2002, I was asked to visit the area but hesitated, as the government's perennial and well-intended efforts to "save" the region often resulted in unkept promises and disappointment. When I couldn't delay the request any longer, I finally agreed to visit the area, but with a determination to avoid overpromising and communicating false hope.*

In addition to meeting leaders, a significant part of my three-day visit was spent visiting people in the community who lived in the worst conditions. The first Colonia *I visited consisted of deteriorated streets lined with a variety of makeshift and dilapidated homes interspersed with mobile and motor homes. Although a number of dwellings looked uninhabitable, we knew they were being lived in, as we saw women hanging clothes to dry or children playing in the dirt. We talked to one family living in a trailer and discovered that this had been their home for several years. They told us they cooked their meals outside on a firepit, and when the weather turned hot (which in South Texas is at least nine months of the year), the children would go to the library until it closed to escape the* overbearing heat. We visited other families who had outhouses for bathrooms and stored drinking water in the same kind of barrels I have seen used in rural areas of Central America.

As we neared the end of our three-day tour, I'll never forget visiting the Gomez family. Their home, although modest and in need of much repair, was made of cinder block and had a fenced-in yard where there were patches of grass and a few plants.

After we exchanged a few pleasantries, we were led into the living room, which was sparsely furnished with one old brown sofa and a small black-and-white television (rabbit ears included) that sat on a barstool. Using the creative and resourceful talents common to families of limited means, the Gomez family had covered their unfinished walls with magazine pictures, cartoon strips, and other scenic pictures that not only brought color to their home but also served as a reminder of their dreams.

From the living room I was led into the "kitchen" where pots and dishes were stacked on a plywood counter. Everything was clean, but it looked to be a mess because there wasn't a cabinet or pantry for storage. As we walked out of the kitchen through a screen door, we entered the real kitchen, where a grill, a burner, and a barrel of water were located. The Gomez kitchen had not been wired for electricity or gas, so they made their meals outside under the tin roof of their carport. Mr. Gomez lost his construction job because of an injury, so from his makeshift kitchen, he made hot meals and sold them from a cart he pushed through the neighborhood.

We went back into the house and entered the bedroom of the family's two young boys. The bare walls of their room were also creatively wallpapered but included the sons' many certificates of achievement and educational honors. Their room had only a full bed (which they shared) and a shelf of books—no computer or video games.

Curiosity got the best of me as we neared the end of our visit. As I had walked through the home, I had noticed hundreds of three-by-five index cards interspersed among the magazine cutouts and pictures on the walls. I took a closer look at the index cards and discovered they were filled with various scripture verses in Spanish. Mr. Gomez saw me looking at the cards and told me the scriptures gave his family hope and guidance. I asked him which was his favorite scripture and expected him to respond with a type of verse that speaks to triumph through adversity or maybe hope for a better future. Instead, Señor Gomez responded, "Jehovah es mí pastor, y nada me faltará"/"The Lord is my Shepherd, I have everything I need."

I was stunned at Señor Gomez's answer. By most material measures, the Gomez family had nothing. Their home was simple, barely providing shelter from the elements. He was disabled and couldn't maintain a steady job. Yet, in the midst of what appeared to be a very bleak situation, the Gomez family understood God's sufficiency, and in His grace, they had peace, hope, and joy. If offered a better circumstance, I'm *sure they'd take it, but they didn't need better circum-stances to be found faithful.*

While I admit to not fully comprehending this kind of faith, I've become convinced that the poor and mar-ginalized have a very special relationship with God. I pray that my family and I can come to know God in the same way the Gomez family members—and many millions of Christians in the developing regions of our world—know Him. I pray that my faith would not be determined by how much I have or don't have so that I would always be able to say, "Jehovah es mí pastor y nada me faltará."—LTC

LA LIBERTAD

For many years I was privileged to speak at a Hispanic student leadership conference in Idaho with an emphasis on math and the sciences. Every year I visited this conference, I felt energy and enthusiasm for leadership, friendships, and the future. Students shared with me their stories of fear and challenges. Most of them grew up in poverty, children of immigrants working in potato fields. Most of these parents pushed them to *"estudiar, porque el estudio es libertad"*/ "study, because education is freedom."

One year I met a young immigrant high school student working toward *la libertad*. She had experienced a tough life, but as many children of immigrants know, the backbreaking work they and their families experience provides a foundation for a strong family. *"Mi padre dice que el trabajo hace que uno tenga carácter"*/ "My father says hard work will build character," she was taught.

Upon arriving in the United States with no money, the young girl's family made their home in a migrant camp close to the fields where they worked. The living conditions varied from abandoned school buses to substandard houses where two or three families resided. The best homes actually had plumbing and running water. She described her environment as temporary and the first of many steps toward a better life.

In spite of the hope for a better future, every day was a challenge. Her family would wake up early, work in the fields, eat, and then the children would walk to school, *"Recuerden, libertad"*/"Remember, liberty" were the send-off remarks from her parents. After school, the children were back in the fields until the sun went down, and then homework began.

After a long day of school and working in the fields, they returned to their humble homes and, lit only by the light of a kerosene lamp, began their last task of the day in completing their school work. Without a computer or printer, they had a bench for a desk, some pencils and paper, and a window to look through and dream of their future.

"If only I can get into college, *la libertad,"* she told me as we talked after a workshop.

This young woman's attitude and academic performance was noticed by her teachers. Impressed with her high marks, her teachers often asked her to stay after school to join clubs, tutor students, or simply assist them with their work, but she declined. Her responsibility was in the fields with her family working together to earn enough money to move into a home.

The following year, I was again invited to speak at this conference. I looked forward to catching up with the students' lives and hearing about the goals they had achieved. There were at least 1,000 students attending, and I could feel a renewed sense of excitement. The young woman from the fields was selected to introduce me. Again, I was honored by her humble story and kindness. She made some general announcements and then asked me if she could take a few minutes to share some news with the other students. *"Claro, mija"*/"Of course, *mija"* (a term of endearment that loosely translates as "my daughter").

As the young girl stood with great pride, she pulled an envelope out of her book bag and unfolded it very slowly. She asked the students to listen carefully because her news was very important.

"Because of your excellent academic achievements," she read, "the Bill Gates Foundation is proud to inform you that you have been awarded a Gates Millenium Scholarship." The crowd went wild with applause and cheers, celebrating the achievement of one of their own. Asking for permission to read another letter, she once again stood tall and began to read, "Congratulations. Because of your academic excellence and commitment to community service, we hereby offer you admittance to Harvard University." Another roar filled the room, as students jumped up and down, energized by the triumph of hard work and diligence, almost as if the acceptance letter had been directed to them personally. I couldn't have been more proud if she had been my own daughter.

I learned many years later that she continued her education, received a PhD, and teaches at the University of California, Davis. I envy those students who sit in her classroom. Her dedication to exploring and achieving all one is destined to become will no doubt contribute to a new generation of students. They will benefit from the fruit of perseverance through struggle—*la libertad*. Freedom can be for all of us.——*LGG*

As we enjoy the liberty to pursue our dreams, it's not easy, but it is a worthwhile endeavor. What is impressive about this young woman is that she shared her story without contempt or anger. At a time when our children demand name brands, complain about chores, and are embarrassed about their parents, this young woman saw her life full of possibility. I am motivated to encourage, support, and be a champion for those who pursue la libertad.——LTC

Looking Beyond Our Past

In my grandmother's hometown, Nueva Rosita, every-one knew each other very well. They knew what they were doing, where they were going, and all the *chisme/* gossip that was available. My aunt, Tia Chonita, cared for my grandmother for years, but as my grand-mother's needs increased, my aunt knew she needed additional help.

Tia Chonita began asking around town to find out if there was anyone who might be available to assist her. Someone mentioned a young woman who was avail-able to work but had suffered abuse in her life, was homeless, and impoverished. Although Tia Chonita didn't know her, because of the urgency of the situa-tion, she sent word for the young woman to meet her. Tia Chonita was reserved and formal, and when she heard someone banging on the door, she was alarmed. There on the doorstep was a rowdy girl with unruly, curly hair nestled on top of her head yelling, *"Señora, ya llegé, abra"/*"Ma'am, I'm here, open." My aunt quickly opened the door, invited her in, and asked her to lower her voice. *"Niña, calmate"*/"Young girl, calm down," she said. *"Soy Rosamaria!"*/"I'm Rosamaria!" the young girl exclaimed. She twirled around and in a high-pitched voice said in Spanish, "It's just that I'm here to work. What do you think?" She glanced around my aunt's house and continued, "Wow, you have TV!"

Tia Chonita had worked very hard as a nurse in a US border town two hours from her small Mexican community. She would work as a nurse one week, and then come home to care for her mother the next. For years she had kept up this routine, and as a result, she had been able to build a nice home for my grandmother. It wasn't extravagant, but she did have a few advantages that others didn't have, such as a television. The young woman looked around as though she'd hit the lottery. *"Que padre la casita, yo me quedo"*/"Nice house, I'll stay," she said, naïve to the fact that the decision was not hers to make.

The two sat while my aunt began to learn about this young woman's heartbreaking life. She was abandoned as a baby, and as a young child she had been passed from home to home, experiencing unspeakable physical and emotional abuse. She had never attended school regularly. "I hear you work hard and you do well," Rosamaria blurted out. "I would have loved to have lived in a family like this." Attracted by the young woman's honesty and simplicity, my aunt hired her, and the two agreed upon employment, responsibilities, and pay.

The young woman was elated to be living with a family, *la familia* Gonzalez. As months went by, Rosamaria proved to be hardworking, a great cook, very loving, and nurturing to my grandmother. As a reward for a job well done, my aunt enrolled Rosamaria in a sewing class, bought her a sewing kit, material, and dress patterns. She was ecstatic and looked forward to the days she would walk the six blocks into town for her sewing class. She felt she now had a family and was learning a new skill. She felt blessed.

She made friends in her sewing classes, and along with Tia Chonita's nieces, Rosamaria attended local dances. At one dance Rosamaria saw a boy who caught her eye. He was handsome, tall, and had dreamy eyes. She thought to herself, *"¿Como le ago para que me vea?"/* "How do I get this boy to notice me?" She did what she did naturally: she giggled! As she and her dance partner got closer to the boy with the dreamy eyes, she giggled long enough to finally catch his attention.

Rosamaria sat down, and immediately the boy with the dreamy eyes came over to introduce himself. *"¿Como te llamas?"/*"What's your name?" he asked. She told him her name, and he asked who she "belonged to." She thought for a moment, then quickly responded, *"la familia* Gonzalez." He probed to find out which *"familia* Gonzalez," and then breathed a sigh of relief as he discovered she came from a good, studious family. He himself was an engineer in the coal-mining industry and came from an established and successful family that was highly admired and respected.

When she came home that night, Rosamaria gave my aunt a detailed overview of the dance and the new boy she'd met. "He liked me!" she concluded with confidence.

The love story continued as the young man became interested in this vivacious, larger-than-life caregiver. She was everything he was looking for—spirited, boisterous, and full of joy. The couple courted for some time but her background was never clearly revealed. One evening, with nerves racing, he asked her to marry him. With a loud *"Ajúa,"* she answered, *"Pues claro que si"*/"But of course." He told her he would speak with her family the following day to ask for her hand in marriage (an old tradition still practiced in many Latin American countries).

Upon hearing the news of this pending proposal, my aunt was stunned. *"¿Le dijiste toda tu historia y que no eres una Gonzalez?"*/"Did you tell him all of your history and that you are not a Gonzalez?" She encouraged Rosamaria to be honest and tell the young man everything about her past. The young girl cried all night knowing that no one would want to marry someone with a past like hers.

The next day, dressed in a suit with polished shoes, and flowers for whom he thought was the mother of the future bride, this handsome young man arrived at Tia Chonita's door. He began to express his love for the young woman, and as he got to the final stage in his request for her hand in marriage, Tia Chonita interrupted him. Together, Tia Chonita and Rosamaria as if mother and daughter, began to share her horrific life journey and described *familia* Gonzalez as her saving grace. When they finished, the young man stood up and walked over to look out the window, his face somber. Rosamaria knew it was over as he would never bring disgrace to his family by marrying her.

After a minute that seemed like eternity, the young man turned from the window with tears streaming down his face and brokenly said, *"Como fue que una muchacha como tu pudo sobrevivir todo eso, tu no lo merecías"*/"How could a young girl overcome all of that, you didn't deserve it," he said. *"Te quiero mas que nunca y me quiero casar contigo y darte la familia que nunca tuviste"*/"I love you more than ever and want to marry you and give you the family you never had." In her spirited way, the caregiver jumped up and ran to him shouting, "Yes, yes, and absolutely yes. I will marry you TODAY!"

And they did marry. My grandmother's young caregiver entered a new world filled with fancy parties, travel, and a family that she now calls her own. "You can hurt my physical being but you can never destroy my soul" was the motto that has kept her strong and focused. She is now a savvy businesswoman, a hostess like no other, and a mother to three children who have all excelled and flourished by living in a family of love. Her greatest teacher, friend, and coach has always been that young dreamy-eyed man she met at the dance.

And although she was initially dismissed and discounted by her new family, she won them over with her robust personality and spirit. Today when her in-laws visit, it is to partake in her loving spirit, family, and home. When I visit my *comadre*, I am amazed at how much she has evolved. But there is still a glimpse of the young spirited girl who now makes me giggle, and I love her all the more.——*LGG*

What a beautiful story that highlights resiliency and perseverance, grace, and love. Resiliency and perseverance in the young girl who, in spite of her experiences, was not paralyzed by shame or fear but was willing to "step up" into a new opportunity. Grace was exhibited in that Tia Chonita, and the young man and soon-to-be husband did not allow artificial barriers of status and class to prevent them from knowing Rosamaria's true beauty.

As my life's career has been in and around the marginalized, I've often heard references to "a lost generation." In most cases, they are referring to those teens and young adults who are like the young caregiver. They are youth disconnected from stable environments and/or institutions, they've often experienced abuse and violence, and they know abandonment too well. Yet, like the caregiver, there are some who have not been permanently "lost" as their life's trajectory has

shifted 180 degrees. One friend, Malissa G., was without a stable home life and lived with more than 45 families as a young girl. She was never part of the child welfare system, but she referred to the people she stayed with as "foster families." Although she was not always in the best of environments, she says, "By God's grace, I always had shelter." Malissa G. is now a wife and mother and is pursuing her PhD in one of our country's top colleges in community development. Another friend, Pastor Natividad Mendoza, has fists tattooed with the words "State Raised" because he spent most of his adolescent and young adult years in California's prison system. Natividad, a man who was considered a "lifer" (he had multiple sentences that would take the entirety of his life to complete), is now a husband, father, and leader of a nonprofit organization called Gangs to Jobs that helps at-risk young men and women destined for destruction change their trajectory to a good future through caring relationships, life skills development, and career placement. Like Rosamaria, Malissa G., and Natividad, there are countless powerful individuals whose lives could not have been imagined as they are today, testifying that the past doesn't have to dictate one's future. Personal history of pain and difficulty can be converted to one that gives our children an inheritance of life, hope, and love.
—LTC

DEVOTION

My Tio Toño was one of the most beloved men I remember. He had a warm, loving face with a magnetic personality that attracted children and adults alike. I recall a day at a wedding where all my little cousins were fidgeting in their seats or running around in circles on the dance floor. When Tio Toño entered the hall through the double doors, like concert-goers who rushed the stage, a swarm of children ran to him with open arms. "Tio Nono!" exclaimed the little ones who were just learning to speak and couldn't quite pronounce his name. The teens tried to hide their enthusiasm but also were eager to reach him, to give him a pat on the back and say *"Que tal, mi Tio Toño"/*"Hey there, my Uncle Toño."

He gave his attention to each child, knowing each of their individual interests and current activities. This was no small feat for an uncle of sixty nephews and nieces.

When I found out Tio Toño was coming from Mexico to the United States to spend the summer with us, my brother and I were overjoyed and relished the thought of having Tio Toño all to ourselves. The envy of all our cousins, we would play, read, and just enjoy him. For us, there was no age or gender barrier—simply a loving, genuine connection.

Needless to say, we were disappointed when we found out Tio Toño was not going to be able to spend all his time with us. His nine growing children had dreams of going to college, so leaving his job as a carpenter, he came to work so that he could provide for them.

Leaving at sunrise with my father every morning, Tio Toño worked eighteen-hour days as a kitchen helper at the restaurant where my dad was a cook. With this heavy work schedule, it was rare that he had time to play with us. My mom, as often is the custom in Latino culture, became his sister, confidant, and mother. On his days off, Mom would cook a *caldo*/soup that reminded him of his family. I can recall him eating a big bowl of *caldo* with so much *chile* that it made his forehead sweat—evidence that the steaming bowl of *caldito*, with its *carne de res, elote, papas, arroz y tortillas de maiz*, was a flavor that was not only delicious but somehow helped him feel closer to home.

I treasured those meals and special moments where, even though he was exhausted, Tio Toño would make us laugh at the dinner table. I could tell he was tired, and he would say, *"Tengo que trabajar duro, mis hijos cuentan conmigo y nos los decepcionaré"*/"I have to work hard, my kids are counting on me, and I can't disappoint them." My father and uncle were happy to work, even if it meant washing dishes, sweeping or mopping at the restaurant—no task was beneath them. This work was the means to their families' future.

The restaurant was in the mountains, some distance from home, in a secluded and wealthy area. Famous people of the time ate there, such as John Wayne, Ronald Reagan, Lee Marvin, and Doris Day. But at night the area seemed so isolated my mother worried about them being far from our little community.

On one evening, as we prepared to have dinner with my Tio, there was a somber feeling at the table. As usual, Tio was sweating from his bald spot and savoring the meal, but I noticed tears of sadness in his eyes. As I looked at him more carefully, I realized he had bruises and cuts all over his body. My first reaction was fear. What had happened? When I inquired, my mother looked over at me and gave me a firm *"Shhh, los niños no hacen preguntas"*/"Shhh, children don't ask questions." So I was quiet and acted as if nothing was wrong.

The next day my Tio did not go to work with my dad, which had become the custom. I knew something was surely wrong because Tio always went to work. He never missed a day. This was serious. All sorts of explanations raced through my mind as I watched my Tio continue to be as somber and sad as he was the previous night at dinner.

Again I asked, *"¿Que pasa, porque nadie nos dice nada?"*/"What's going on? Why won't anyone tell us anything?" My Tio heard the fear in my voice and told me, *"No te preocupes, estoy bien"*/"Don't worry, I'm OK." But I knew better.

Tio went back to work after a couple of days, but the sadness lingered in our home. That same day an aunt came to visit, and reading my mother's emotions, she asked what was wrong. I was planted at the table to hear my mother's response when she sent me away, again preventing me from learning what was happening. Clearly, my mother was doing all she could to save me from grief.

From my bedroom, I heard my mother begin to cry. She told my aunt that a few evenings before, the restaurant where my dad and Tio worked had been robbed. There were only a few workers at the time, and Tio had taken the brunt of the violence. They taped his mouth shut, tied him to a chair, and beat him severely. The men robbing the restaurant asked for money, and when Tio's reply was *"No hablo inglés"*/"I don't speak English," they struck him violently again and again.

I began to cry. My poor dear Tio. Didn't they know he was the nicest, kindest, most gentle man ever? How could anyone do this to him? I was angry and disturbed by what I heard. I cried myself to sleep that night, not understanding this cruelty.

The next day I saw my Tio defeated, a bit sore, and his steps did not have the same swing. He entered my room and shot me a forced smile. I jumped out of my bed and said, *"¿Como estas, Tio, te puedo ayudar?"/* "How are you, Uncle? Can I help you?" He gave me a light hug, his soreness preventing our customary full embrace. I told him I knew what had happened and that I was worried about him. He told me he was fine and for me not to worry, but I asked him if he would return to Mexico sooner than planned, as this seemed to be the logical next step, given the trauma that he experienced. He looked straight into my eyes and said, *"Hija, en ese momento sufrí mucho, pero solo pense en mi hijos y como mi familia me necesita"/*"Honey, in that moment I suffered greatly, but I only thought of my kids and how much my family needs me." He continued, *"Sobrevivi por ellos"/*"I survived for them." He knew his work was helping his family build a better future.

I had loved Tio Toño before, but now I honored him. His devotion to his family was hard for me to comprehend as a little girl who was naïve about the love parents feel for their children. In looking back, I now understand and hold without judgment the love of a parent who would suffer through any challenge, struggle, or pain for their children. The darkness in our home was eventually alleviated and returned to the joy we always felt with Tio Toño. At the end of that summer, we reluctantly said our goodbyes, and our beloved uncle returned to his *familia*.

Tío Toño is no longer alive, but he left behind an inheritance of hard work that continues. His children include physicians, engineers, nurses, educators, successful businessmen, and even a professional singer and entertainer on radio, television, and in our own family.—*LGG*

Not too long ago my daughter and I had the opportunity to travel to El Salvador on a service trip. On this trip, I took some extra time to visit the work of World Vision and ENLACE, two organizations focused on community development. On my last day of visiting different project sites, I had the opportunity to meet children ages nine through twelve in an afterschool program. These children were curious about me as an American of Hispanic descent who spoke both English and Spanish. As we talked and I learned of their stories, I remember seeing a thin, frail girl that was the size of an eleven-year-old but had a mature face. As the kids moved out to the playground, this young girl watched them from the side, quietly smiling and laughing while she carried a nine-month-old baby that looked like he weighed more than she did. As I looked at the girl, I noticed her eyes. For lack of a better term, she had a haunted, sad, and empty look. She reluctantly allowed one of the American visitors to hold the baby while she joined the kids and played—but she quickly came back to take the baby. We

learned later that this fourteen-year-old girl had a twelve-year-old brother and a baby brother—the one she was carrying. Not too long before our visit, her mother and father had left for the United States to work, while she and her siblings were put in the care of her neighbors. In learning this story, we had so many questions without sufficient answers. Was the young girl being treated well? Who was taking care of her well-being? Was she being supported in her education? How could the parents abandon their children?

When we see immigrants in the United States, like Tío Toño, little do we understand the sacrifice, pain, desperation, and heartache experienced not only by those who have left their family, but also by the family left behind.—LTC

La Loca and the Sneetches

Growing up in California was perfect for me, as I was able to spend long days at the beach or at the community swimming pool splashing in the water and absorbing the sun.

As is still the case in many parts of the world today, when I was young, light skin seemed to be revered in our family. When a baby was born, it was as if someone hit the lottery when they proudly announced their newborn had very light skin. Unfortunately, the opposite was true when a baby with dark skin was born. In a not-so-happy tone people said, *"Pobrecita, esta bien morenita"*/"Poor thing, she's really dark." Although these messages were never meant with malice, at an early age I learned that light skin was favored.

When I was twelve, we moved to a new, mostly white neighborhood where, to my surprise, I discovered that being blond and tanned was desirable. I was one for two as I wasn't blond but I certainly had a tan—I was born with it! As the summer arrived, most of my new friends were planning on making their hair more blond and their skin dark. I, on the other hand, had other priorities. I just wanted to enjoy swimming and have fun. Even though we always had difficulty waking up early for school, as soon as summer started, my brother and I hopped out of bed, ready to go for the first community pool session, which started at 9:00 a.m. sharp. At the noon break, we would eat our packed lunch and wait for the second session to begin at 1:00 p.m.

After weeks of swimming, my mom began to worry about my ever-changing skin color, saying that I was getting too dark. While I knew racism and discrimination existed in our communities, I didn't understand why I couldn't spend more time in the pool. *"Le prometo, Ma, me pongo gorra y camiseta pa no quemarme"*/"I promise, Mom, I will wear a hat and T-shirt to not burn," I told my mother. I was having fun. It didn't matter to me if I was getting dark—I couldn't give up the sun and water.

Directly across the street from us lived a very eccentric woman who seemed to share my love for the sun. She *always* wore a two-piece bikini around her house. She mowed her front lawn in a bikini, trimmed her flowers in a bikini, and even stood outside in a bikini to call her kids to dinner. As far as I could tell, it seemed that she wore a bikini twenty-four hours a day. This six-foot-tall, bikini-clad woman was striking, shapely, and had long blond hair she wore in two braids. Our kitchen window faced her house, and my parents would often look out that window and be in shock with what they saw. *"Esa señora esta loca, siempre encuerada"*/"That woman is crazy, always naked," my parents would say, nicknaming her *La Loca*.

As the summer wore on, I became intrigued with this woman who seemed to do all she could to catch the sun's rays. While I was constantly being told to cut back on my pool time, she was splashing herself with baby oil and sizzling in the sun, doing everything she could to get darker.

One day while kicking a ball around in our front yard, I crossed the street and came face to face with *La Loca*. Of course, she was in her bikini and covered in baby oil. "Hi," she said. "You're my daughter's friend. You go swimming with her at the community pool, right?" I answered "yes" a bit cautiously as well as frightened by the woman I heard was *loca*.

"What are you doing?" I asked. She sat up, with her gorgeous blond hair reflecting the sun. I continued, "I see you every day out here, just laying on this towel. Why?" With no hesitation and a beautiful smile she responded, "Because I want to look like you." She what? This was puzzling. Did I hear her correctly? This sun goddess wanted to look like me? "I sit out every day, splash on this baby oil by the gallon, and spend hours in the sun to achieve your skin color. You're beautiful!" I was both confused and excited as she told me I was beautiful because I was dark! I couldn't wait to tell my mom.

Those affirming words have had a lasting impact on me. Indeed, I was beautiful in my God-given brown skin. I was born with the tan other people spend hours (and risk getting cancer) trying to achieve. *La Loca* helped me recognize that my skin color does not define me, but is a unique aspect of my identity.—*LGG*

Early in my professional career at Bank of America, I was given a Dr. Seuss book called The Sneetches. *The Sneetches was about two types of yellow birds: the ones with the stars and the ones without stars. They live out the age-old story too often repeated—looking down on someone, or alternatively, looking up to someone, because of the way their appearance. Initially, the Green-Star-Bellied Sneetches were fashionable—they were the "in" crowd—and the envy of the Starless Sneetches. Along comes an entrepreneurial fellow who devises a "Star-On" machine that was a huge success as all the Starless Sneetches purchased a star. Now all the Sneetches looked alike with a green star planted firmly on their chest. The original star bearers didn't like that they were no longer the elite. In enters the entrepreneur again, now getting rich on the "Star-Off" machine because the original green-star-bellied Sneetches now wanted to look different! All the Sneetches switch back and forth between machines until they have spent all their money trying to change their appearance.*

La Loca and the Sneetches remind us that it doesn't matter whether we have dark skin or light, or have full lips or flat hips. From the womb, we've been made beautiful, wonderful, and with a purpose.—LTC

SHARED FAMILY DREAMS

I have had the privilege of being included among the speakers of the United States Hispanic Leadership Institute, a large national conference that over the last thirty years has helped develop amazing national Latino leaders.

To highlight the valiant sacrifices made by our families so that we can enjoy a better life, I include in my talk the stories of those, who with fear and difficulty, struggled to cross the Rio Grande River or the Arizona desert. As my father used to say, *"Por ti, hija, por tu futuro"*/"For you, daughter, for your future." He would continue. "We have come to this country and all we ask is that you study. Become someone."

Often students come to meet me after a presentation, and sometimes they share personal stories of triumph; at other times, they need a hug and affirmation that someone understands their pain. One year, I saw a young man who kept allowing others to go before him so that he could be at the end of the line—as if he wanted private time with me. As his turn finally came, this six-foot, 250-pound young man stepped up respectfully and engulfed me in a big hug. As he held me tight, I knew he was crying. I said nothing and held still; somehow I knew that at that moment, I was playing the role of his mother.

Finally, after an extended embrace, he released me and, without embarrassment or apology, proceeded to tell me his story. He said his parents immigrated to the United States some twenty-five years earlier and that he was a US citizen by birth. He lived here with his parents and siblings, while the remainder of his family—his aunts, uncles, cousins, and grandparents—all lived in Mexico.

He said he was happy to be graduating from college in three months, but as I asked how his parents would celebrate his graduation, his tears began to fall again as he said, *"Mis papis fueron deportados a Mexico"*/"My parents have been deported to Mexico. They were sent back. I always thought they were citizens, and since I was born here I just assumed . . ." His voice trailed off.

His family, he said, had been separated in the moment of their greatest accomplishment, the achievement of his parents' dream, a college education for their son. He talked with them every day, and he said that they would be front row and center to witness their dream come true through their son's graduation. I wondered how that might be possible, but didn't question him. He said they had already twice attempted to return by swimming across the Rio Grande River, pleading when they got caught only to have the chance to see their son graduate from college. They were not giving up, determined to be with their son on this day of achievement. I don't know if this young man's parents saw their son graduate, but whether they were present or not, they could be proud their son realized their family's dream.——*LGG*

Permanently fixing the complicated and broken immigration system has been a task volleyed back and forth over the years for lack of courage. At stake are not only the dreams of children of immigrants, but also the dreams of mothers and fathers who have exhibited uncommon courage and uncommon strength to achieve the dream shared by all parents: a better future for their children.——LTC

WOMEN AHEAD OF THEIR TIME

There are many *mujeres*/women who have been examples of remarkable stamina, discipline, intelligence,
and creativity. Often we fail to see these extraordinary
talents within our own family because they don't always fit within the mainstream definition of success or
triumph. For me, the women in my family have been
my chief role models and teachers. They continue to
inspire me today.

Ma Almita

Ma Almita, my husband's grandmother, was born in
the early 1900s and grew up in a small ranch town in
South Texas. She graduated from high school and was
accepted at a prestigious Texas college—one of the few
women, let alone Hispanic women, in her era to have
this opportunity. At nearly 100, she still tells us how
she challenged the boys at school to see who could
race home and be the first to start chopping wood. Of
course she would always win to prove that girls could

be just as good as boys at school, racing, chopping wood, as well as housework!

After I received my PhD I visited with my family and spent a lovely afternoon at her house. As always she was preparing a great meal that included every individual's favorite dish, managing the entire menu with ease. I became thirsty and walked to the refrigerator for a cold drink. As I opened the refrigerator door I was shocked at what I saw.

"Ma Almita," I called, walking back into the living room, "You know I now have a PhD," I continued with a know-it-all tone in my voice.

"*Sí, mija,* you are very smart," she gently responded.

"I'm worried about your health, Ma Almita. Come with me to the refrigerator so I can explain," I said.

She followed me to the kitchen, and I opened the refrigerator door. "Look how you are eating," I said with a pompous attitude, waving my hand up and down at shelves filled with artificial whipped cream containers. "You're eating far too much unhealthy food. It's filled with sugar, fat, and empty calories."

A smile spread across Ma Almita's beautiful round, full face, and with a kind, sweet voice she told me to open the containers in the refrigerator. I looked at her with a puzzled expression and began to lift each lid. The bowls were filled with *chorizo con huevo, Fideo,* and other leftovers.

Without judging or embarrassing me, Ma Almita gently explained, "When we bake cakes for the church, we make our icing with whipped cream, then we keep the bowls and reuse them for storage. We can't afford fancy plastic storage dishes." She was being environmentally friendly and didn't even know it!

It was a simple lesson reminding me to stay humble in spite of my achievements. We can always learn from creative, resourceful women!

Choco

Maria del Socorro (Choco), my mother, has many talents, but her first priority has always been to be the best wife and mom possible, never wavering from her responsibilities. To this day, as she approaches eighty, she and my dad go to the senior citizen's gym and work out five days a week. She belongs to church groups and holds officer positions in some ministries. She gardens, cooks, cleans, and cares for her home.

And Mom is a masterful hairstylist. Among our family and within our neighborhood she became well known for her elaborate up-dos, arranging piles of hair in beautiful buns and swirls on top of each head. Everyone wanted my mom to style her hair. *"Choco, peíname bien bonita que voy a un baile"*/"Do my hair really nice because I'm going to a dance," my aunts would often say.

Many people encouraged her. *"Debes estudiar, tienes mucho talento"*/"You should go to beauty school. You have so much talent." My mom wanted to study, but didn't know how she could go about this since she hadn't finished high school in Mexico.

With some assistance from a translator, my mother did finish beauty school. Then, to put her skills to work, my dad built her a beauty shop right in their garage. Yes, the garage! *"Así puedo peinar y hacer de cenar al miso tiempo"*/"That way I can comb hair and make dinner at the same time," she said.

And cook and style she did for more than thirty years. Once she received her state license, there was always someone coming for a color, perm, haircut, or style. On Saturdays my dad often removed paper from perm rods just to help out.

Nothing stood in my mom's way of feeling useful and contributing to our family. She retired at the age of sixty-eight or so, but on any given Saturday you will still find women coming to the house and begging Choco, *"Andale, peíname, nadien lo hace como tu"*/ "Come on, do my hair. No one does it like you."

Polly
Polly, my mother-in-law, grew up looking forward to what she knew would be her primary role—wife and mother. After high school, she married and enjoyed the life she expected until her husband died in a car accident on Mother's Day with gifts for her left behind in the smashed car. A young widow and single mother, Polly was overwhelmed and had no idea how

she could live without her husband and become the primary provider for her two small children.

After a long grieving process, she slowly began to find the power to re-create herself. She knew the best way to support her family would be to get a college degree and enter the workforce. Although it was difficult and slow, with the support of her family, she received her teaching degree on the same day her son (my husband) graduated from high school.

After marrying my husband, I came to know Polly as a very dedicated teacher. She continued her education and pursued a master's degree. On the day of her graduation, I sat in the front row and was inspired by her tenacity and sheer will to become the very best teacher for her students. I was in awe of my mother-in-law, older than most graduates but equally accomplished and full of delight. As she crossed the stage, a chill ran up my back because I had never seen an adult woman do such a thing. I wondered if I, too, could do something this special as I had put my education on hold as my family grew. Upon returning to her seat, Polly walked in front of me, and looked directly at me with unspoken words as if to say, "You too can do this. Try!" I was profoundly moved and unable to hold back my tears of emotion and pride. She had communicated something to me, not necessarily in words, but by example. She taught me it's never too late to learn, to grow, and to reach beyond one's wildest expectations.

There and then I made a decision to return to college and eventually obtained bachelor's, master's, and doctorate degrees.

Tia Chonita

My mother's sister, Tia Chonita, is a legend in our family. She was the first in our family to go to college. Unlike most women of the '40s, she left her small town to attend college and became a nurse.

Unfortunately, pay for a nurse in a small town was minimal, so when a labor and delivery nursing position came up in a US border hospital, she immediately took it. She became a favorite among doctors, who asked for her to assist with many baby deliveries.

Tia Chonita would work long shifts for five days and then drive back to her small town in Mexico to care for her mother. For nearly thirty-three years she kept this schedule with the help of caregivers she hired to stay with her mother while she was away.

She mentored many women in our family as well as those young women who worked for her in her home. For me, she offered a vision of possibilities. In addition to her professional accomplishments, she was known to us as the aunt who was able to buy herself a car. And what a car it was! A beautiful aqua-colored, stick-shift Mustang. Tia Chonita would drive through Nueva Rosita, avoiding pot holes and looking cool, dressed in her adorable white uniform.

She was an example for all the women in our family. From her we learned we could be smart and also have great style!—*LGG*

Many of us are surrounded by individuals who are excellent role models. In my own family, I think of Grandma Pepa (great-grandmother), Grandma Mary, and Grandma Menchaca. Each one has a story. Grandma Pepa was my first babysitter when my mother started working, taking care of me and my brother as infants. Although she wasn't able to care for us as we grew older, she would always go out of her way when we visited her home, taking out the pots to make mole and rice as soon as we arrived.

I remember Grandma Mary as one who was always working on one thing or another. Over the years she had several dogs (usually chihuahuas) that were all named Chiquita (except for a Buffy somewhere in there). She loved to play church songs on the piano, and on Sundays, one could always find her at the little neighborhood church, of which she was a member most of her life.

Then there was my Grandma Menchaca, my maternal grandmother, always ready to share a funny story. As a pastor's wife, she maintained a nonstop schedule as she organized programs, events, and meals in the church. I have a few notebooks of hers that have her notes from the Bible classes she taught. In the middle of these deep spiritual insights, I'd find her notes on the Christmas gifts she was going to give to each of my forty-or-so cousins. It's nice to know that the gifts she gave us were written next to the notes on the eternal gifts she would speak about in church. Until her dying day she gave us Christmas gifts, birthday gifts, and a gift "just because." And she was always ready to share a piece of gum or candy she carried in her purse. The greatest gift she gave us was herself.

The daughters of my grandmothers—Licha, Maya, Sylvia, Elsa, Dianne, and Mirta—have all lived lives of inspiration, devotion, faith, and humor.

Finally, there is my mom, la linda Linda. Who can do justice writing about one's mom? Certainly not me. Suffice it to say she is one of the smartest and most resourceful individuals I know, not to mention stylish, contemporary, and outgoing. She is always ready for a party and doesn't let much slow her down. Her energy beats mine, and her fearlessness has no match. She doesn't know the impossible. With all of this zeal and energy, she is also one who generously serves others as she cares for those who are unable to care for themselves. I can only hope I live up to the standard she has set.——LTC

GUATEMALAN ANGEL

When I travel on business trips, I have come to appreciate that airplanes take me to destinations and experiences I might otherwise not have. Never was this more true than on the morning I boarded my first flight from San Antonio to Houston en route to North Carolina.

It was spring break, and hundreds of families with young children were traveling to fun-filled destinations. I boarded my early flight sleepy and a bit grumpy after a very intense and busy weekend. I saw a few rows of young Latino boys sitting straight and tall, not like any of the other spirited kids on the plane. I sat down in my aisle seat next to one of the Latino boys, smiled, and said hello. He responded with a brief smile. "How rude," I thought, sending my last email before turning off my phone. Although I wanted to be quiet, close my eyes, and relax for the forty-five-minute flight, something made me reach out to this boy. *"Que tal"/*"Hi there," I said. I could see his eyes were cold and tired. He smiled again but didn't say another word.

Despite his demeanor, I noticed something tender about this boy and persisted with a conversation. I asked him where he was going, and in Spanish he timidly told me he was traveling to Houston to live. I immediately started filling him in on information about Houston, the weather, the size of the city, and other facts. "Where are you from?" I asked, to which he told me Guatemala. "Oh, that's a long flight," I said. *"No vine en avion, llegé caminando"*/"I didn't come in a plane, I came walking," he said. I was shocked at his response, not really sure if I understood him correctly. As I looked at him with some confusion, he took my hand and began to tear up.

In Spanish he told me he was in a group of boys who had walked more than 1,500 miles from Guatemala to the border of Texas. At first I thought he was joking, but his serious face communicated honesty and pain. While crossing the Rio Grande River, the boys were apprehended. Half were returned to Guatemala because they were older than eighteen, and the remainder were sent to a detention center in San Antonio. Even though he was basically under lock and key, he said his time in San Antonio was almost like a vacation compared to the life he left behind. In San Antonio he was treated well and was allowed to eat and play outside. Now traveling to a detention center in Houston, he hoped to connect with family members he thought lived there.

"I lost my mother a few years ago, and I was orphaned because my father abandoned me. I have lived alone and have suffered much," he said, explaining that he was much younger than his seventeen siblings, some of whom now lived in the United States. In the middle of our heart-wrenching conversation, he happened to look out the window, and realizing we were flying, he almost jumped out of his seat and turned to me with wonder in his voice, exclaiming, "It's my first time on a plane!" For a split second, I saw him separated from his pain and realized he was a normal sixteen-year-old on his first plane ride.

He continued his story, saying he felt alone. "I do have one friend who has walked with me. He is Jesus. He has never abandoned me," the boy said with tears streaming down his face. I began to offer words of comfort and shared the story of my own father's journey of coming to this unfamiliar country and finding a better life. I told the boy I wished the same for him too.

Toward the end of the flight, I gave him my business card, assuring him I would help him in any way I could. He looked into my eyes and asked me if I had something to write with as he wanted me to call his sister who lived in Houston, to assure her he was OK. When I told him I was traveling to North Carolina, he was overjoyed. *"Ahí vive mi hermano, si lo ve por favor dele un abrazo y decirle que estoy bien"*/"My brother lives there, if you see him, give him a hug for me." Although it was highly unlikely I would run into his brother in North Carolina, I responded, *"Claro que sí"*/"Yes, of course."

Our arms were locked and tears ran down our faces as we quietly sat for the remaining fifteen minutes of the flight. For those few minutes, he was my son and I his mother. Nothing else mattered in that moment. I tried to lighten the mood at some point, and asked if I could see his name tag. He handed it to me. On the front was his name and some numbers, and inserted behind it was a prayer card that had images of Jesus carrying children in His arms. With great emotion and confidence, the boy proclaimed, "He is my strength and He has brought you to me."

I didn't know why I was brought to that aisle seat on a flight from San Antonio to Houston, but I hope I was able to provide love to a young boy experiencing the kind of pain and struggle that many of us only read about. Here was the struggle that had a name, a family, and a future that was uncertain. I also have recognized how often we are disconnected from humanity. On the trip that morning, I could have been so caught up in trivial issues—an early flight, a busy weekend, a challenging work schedule—that I might have easily missed the opportunity to profoundly connect with this young man. The truth was, I needed him as much as he needed me.

Our plane landed, and we were still arm-in-arm. With a tight hug, I said goodbye to him and started to walk down the aisle of the plane. I turned to wave again, and he was on the edge of his seat as if he wanted me to return. I smiled and said goodbye with the hope that one day our paths would cross again.——*LGG*

The practice of "welcoming the stranger" is one that is often lost in our American culture because it usually requires some level of sacrifice. In our comfortable lifestyles, we are prone to avoid anything that may take focus away from our own desires or wants. When Lorena put aside her own interests, she opened the door of her heart and welcomed the stranger by engaging this young Guatemalan boy. Her sacrifice paid unexpected and profound dividends for both her and the boy. When we welcome the stranger, we may be welcoming an angel in disguise.——LTC

The Family We Choose

I was in Washington state, my last stop on a rigorous ten-day trip for a healthy marriage and relationship initiative I was working on. To become acquainted with the background of the participants in the program, I visited the community where they lived. In a matter of just a few minutes, I felt I had walked from one developed, organized, and well-resourced country into a completely different one. I saw dilapidated homes interconnected by dirt roads. There was no grass or vegetation, and the trees that survived looked withered and dead. Many people speak of how the weather of the Great Northwest can take a toll on one's emotional demeanor. I can only imagine the challenges resulting from the combination of gloomy weather and a difficult living environment.

The morning of the focus group I started my day with a quick breakfast and a walk around the picturesque small town where the meeting was to be held. It was a clear contrast to the town where our focus group participants lived. Here, the streets were clean, the buildings freshly painted, and the windows of the shops and stores featured displays of beautiful fruits and vegetables, all of which had been harvested by the migrant workers who lived in the community I had visited the day before.

My purpose for this trip was to engage couples and learn how the family-strengthening program in which they participated affected their relationships with one another and their families. Since the ten couples that volunteered to participate had not had time to eat after work, we started with dinner, which also provided an opportunity for a conversation warm-up.

As the couples arrived, I noticed they were very comfortable with one another, laughing, joking, and having a good time. The women hugged as they greeted one another and the men offered each other their manly *abrazos*/hugs—a true sign of brotherhood. I was sure their comfort with one another resulted from having known each other for a long time—perhaps having immigrated from the same country or even the same town. I started the session by asking each one to introduce themselves; the women usually took on this role for themselves as well as their partners. After each introduction, someone in the group would add an editorial comment about the couple. *"Ellos son como nuestra familia, siempre estan apoyando en todo lo possible"*/"They have been like family, always supporting us whenever possible," one said. *"Mi compá me a ayuda en momentos muy deficiles, somos familia"*/

"My buddy has always helped in moments of great difficulty, we're family," another called out.

Unlike some other focus groups I've conducted, these couples were eager to talk and excited to share their experiences. In a discussion about the way we are raised, the conversation turned serious. In Spanish, one father shared his inability to tell his children he loved them. "In these classes with my family around me, I learned to first say . . . well, to say 'it' to my wife. Sometimes I will say 'it' to my children too," he said. He further explained that he had never been exposed to tender words or demonstrations of love because his parents felt the best way to prepare him for life was to make him a strong and firm man. They felt acts of love would make him weak and too sensitive.

I asked his wife what she thought about her husband's response. She explained that she wanted her children to know their father loved them. "I hurt worse for them than for me. I know he loves me, but I want my children to also know they are loved by him."

Just then another man in the group encouraged his friend to tell his wife he loved her. *"Andele, compá, digale a su mujer que la quiere"*/"Come on, buddy, tell your wife you love her." The room was silent. The man turned to his wife and, apparently for the first time in public, said, *"Te quiero"*/"I love you." With an immediate and resounding cheer, the group broke out in applause.

As we continued with the focus group, I learned that although the family-strengthening program had formally ended, the friendships within this group and sense of community continued. They met regularly at various homes to review and discuss the material they had learned in the program. *"No queremos que se olvide lo que apredimos"*/"We don't want to forget what we have learned."

As many families find themselves in distant and foreign places, they often build friendships that become much like families with whom they connect and grow. In a desolate migrant camp in Washington, not only had these program participants strengthened their relationships, marriages, and families, they had built a strong, nurturing community.—*LGG*

I grew up in an environment that valued community. While technically I had only one set of grandparents and seven aunts and uncles in Houston (where I was raised), there were dozens of families who supported and encouraged me. Referring to the adults in my church as hermanos y hermanas, *these individuals were not only my spiritual family but also my extended, earthly family who always sought out ways to be together. It was not unusual for twenty of us to meet up at the local cafeteria for Sunday lunch or to grab burgers and fries at a nearby restaurant after Friday night*

youth group. Even though we would stay out until very late at night, we made sure that before we ended our night, we had a plan in place to meet at a swimming pool or softball field to spend the next afternoon together.

It was not until I became an adult that I learned this type of community is not common. Also, as an adult, I've realized there are many challenges in our contemporary culture that make it difficult to re-create the type of extended community in which I was raised. Living in the D.C. Metro area away from my Texas family, I've had to find ways to replicate for my children the type of community that surrounded me as a child. I haven't been completely successful, but on some occasions—when we invite our neighbors for a potluck dinner, have an impromptu backyard fire to make s'mores, or gather with other families for special events—my children have experienced a little bit of what it means to have a home away from home, just like the migrant community in Washington. And my children love it!—LTC

MR. JEWELRY

After graduating from high school, I went straight to college. Keeping up academically and financially was difficult, and I began to feel college was not for me. I was barely passing my classes and I had no money. My parents did the best they could, but I felt I needed my own spending money, so I dropped out of college and looked for a job. Other than working at a day care as a teen, I had little experience in the work force and my options were limited. My friend told me about a job at a jewelry store, and while I had no experience in sales, I decided to apply anyway.

I was interviewed by Mr. Jewelry, the manager of the jewelry store. Toward the end of the interview, he told me I would receive a commission on everything I sold. Mr. Jewelry was a heavyset man about the age of my father. Winking, he said, "The sweeter the smile, the better the sale." That made sense to me. I knew that good customer service would help me succeed. I was hired on the spot.

The jewelry store was in downtown San Antonio, an area full of excitement and tourists visiting the Alamo, the Hemisphere Tower, and Riverwalk. It also was an area where large groups of military servicemen visited day and night.

On my first day at the store, Mr. Jewelry said, "If you do a good job like the other girl, maybe the servicemen will also buy you something." I thought this was odd, not quite understanding why I would want jewelry from someone I didn't know. I asked the sales clerk why she received gifts from the servicemen, and how she went about selling so much jewelry. She looked at me, tilted her head, and with a big smile said, "Well, if you look sweet, ease into the counter, and tilt your head a bit, the military guys will go crazy and they don't even know what they're buying. Often they just give it back for me to keep."

I decided to try this approach on the first group of young men who came into the store. They walked directly to me and asked what I'd recommend for their sweethearts back home. Tilt, smile, lean in—that was my game plan. They questioned me about what I liked, and I awkwardly tried to maintain my tilt, smile, and lean-in position while I showed them earrings, bracelets, and a necklace or two. They bought a few pieces and left the store. I made the sale, but instead of being happy, I felt nauseated. This didn't seem right.

Later that day Mr. Jewelry came to congratulate me for doing so well my first day on the job. "You are learning a lot from our number one seller," he said. My stomach began to churn again. He told me to move to the other counter so he could offer me sales advice. I did as I was told, but there was barely enough room for one person to stand behind the counter, let alone two. I began to situate myself—tilt, smile, and lean in—when out of the corner of my eye I saw Mr. Jewelry coming toward me. I thought he was trying to squeeze behind me to get to my other side. I pushed myself against the counter to make room for him to pass, but when he brushed by me, he placed his hands on my behind. My stomach was in knots. I wanted to slap him. I might have been naïve, but I knew this was definitely wrong! *"Don't you ever, and I mean ever, do that again,"* I told him emphatically. The feeling of betrayal and disgust overwhelmed me. I was young enough to be his daughter! I couldn't imagine why he had behaved this way.

In that moment behind the counter, I had a flashback of all the amazing women in my family who always held themselves with dignity and grace. I heard my mother's advice, *"Siempre darte a respetar"*/"Always demand respect." I thought about their examples and love and decided to walk out of the jewelry store with all the drama I had learned in the novelas. I grabbed my belongings, flipped my hair, and said, *"A mi nadien me trata así"*/"No one treats me that way."

As I continued down the street I began to cry—not out of sadness but of victory. I stood tall! I had inherited many strengths from the women in my life, and on that day, I put these strengths into action!—*LGG*

Self-respect is a characteristic all of us must develop. If we don't honor ourselves, who will? Sometimes it's difficult to stand up against people in authority. We've been taught to respect our elders, but we have to remain firm against those who try to take advantage of us. And sometimes, we might even need to stand firm for others who are afraid to raise their voices in protest against injustice.——LTC

THE MEXICAN POWER NAP

Hard work has always been an important value for me in my personal and professional life. I have witnessed members of my family work countless hours to save and provide for their families. I meet men and women throughout the country whose sweat, sunburns, and physical ailments are evidence of the exhausting workloads they endure. Perhaps this is why the stereotypical image of the Sleeping Mexican has offended me for years. The image depicts a Mexican man, shaded from the sun by a large *sombrero*, either barefoot or wearing *huaraches*, with a *zarape* that drapes across his back while he naps next to a cactus.

The Sleeping Mexican is historically the most offensive image in the Mexican American culture. For years, activists protested it by boycotting stores, restaurants, or any other business using it to portray Mexican culture. I recall coming across a Sleeping Mexican lawn fixture one afternoon while visiting a friend in Arizona. I was horrified when my friend said she liked it. "I see this image all the time," she said. She felt validated by the fact that even Mexican restaurants, owned by Mexicans, used this image in their décor.

Months later, my husband and I traveled to Mexico on a short vacation and visited an area being revitalized after hurricanes destroyed the coastline. The drive from the airport to the hotel was lined with hundreds of landscapers and construction workers rebuilding streets and hotels. Once again I saw the labor and hard work of *mi gente,* my people. Later that day as I roamed the streets and shops of the little town where we stayed, I walked into a shop filled with local artisan creation and came face to face with literally thousands of Sleeping Mexican clay figurines. These clay figurines, ranging from one to four feet tall, lined shelf after shelf, along with cloth dolls, wood carvings, and posters of this same Sleeping Mexican.

I was furious! My husband, Rene, moved out of the way as I walked toward the front counter. He knew I was angry, and the expression on his face clearly communicated, "Oh no, here she goes again." I arrived at the front counter with my arms filled with figurines, and a gentleman, Señor Mendoza, asked, *"¿Pa que soy bueno, Señorita?"*/"How can I help, ma'am?" In an authoritative voice I began to tell him how angry I was about the Sleeping Mexican image that he sold by the thousands. *"¿Oiga, porque tan enojada, Señorita?"*/ "Why are you so angry, ma'am?" he asked. I began my pointed and lengthy critique of the emotional and psychological impact this Sleeping Mexican has had on our Mexican community.

With respect and kindness, Señor Mendoza gently smiled and said, *"Pos yo no se lo que usted dice, pero yo aquí adrentro, estoy muy contento con mi trabajito"*/"I don't understand all that you have said, but I am very content with my job indoors." He explained that for forty years he worked fourteen-hour days, six days a week in the grueling hot sun. He joked, *"Yo era blanco, pero con tanto sol me hice prieto"*/"I used to be white but with so much sun I got dark." He continued by saying the years of construction caused problems with his health. His back, legs, and feet allowed him to stand for no more than twenty minutes at the counter, and his breathing was labored as a result of toxic materials used in both construction and the fields.

I responded, *"Por eso me enojó, porque se que muchos trabajan muy duro para que reflejen a un flojo Mexicano durmiendo la siesta"*/"That's why I get so mad because I know how hard many work, and the image of a lazy Mexican at siesta is a poor reflection on who we truly are." In his demure way, he told me I had it all wrong. The image, he said, depicted the simple truth—a man needs a siesta after fourteen hours of backbreaking work! I was stunned as this man's words presented me with a perspective I had never considered. Though I am well traveled, informed, and have taught at the university level on stereotypes and racial issues, I had never heard this interpretation of the Sleeping Mexican.

I collected myself, feeling a bit embarassed for my outrage. I thanked him for his time and purchased some random items (I felt this was the least I could do). As I walked out the door, I recalled the many times my dad had divided his forty-five-minute lunch hour between eating and resting—not because he was lazy, but because he was exhausted from hard work in unbearable temperatures.

I've adjusted my perspective on the Sleeping Mexican. I no longer view it as a racist statement on my culture. While I know some dismiss my new understanding as too simplistic, I believe it reflects the reality of many of our hardworking men and women. The Sleeping Mexican is our hardworking community's version of the executive power nap. Like Señor Mendoza said, everybody needs a nap after hours of backbreaking work!—*LGG*

In recent years, there has been more discussion around the idea of rest. Rest is an ancient concept, even one that is sacred. God Himself rested after six days of work creating our universe!

Rest is certainly the activity modeled by the Sleeping Mexican. For me, it might include a hammock, shade tree, and a light breeze. However, a physical settling down is only part of the rest we need. In our crazy, busy lives, it is important to take time to reflect and be mentally and emotionally recharged and recalibrated so we're not busy running as fast as we can in the wrong direction.

We all need downtime—whether it is on a daily or periodic basis. Although our tendency is to see downtime as unproductive, it really can be the best investment we make for our families and ourselves.—LTC

THE WOMAN IN THE
"NO-ONE-WILL-SEE-ME" OUTFIT

Sharing stories is my passion, and I am blessed to make a living doing what I love even though it is not always easy. The cold, snowy Midwestern morning to which I awoke on one assignment foreshadowed the challenge I would face staying true to my values and culture.

I had been invited to speak at a conference and conduct a half-day workshop to help an accomplished group of individuals better understand the Latino community. I arrived at the hotel in my proverbial "no-one-will-see-me" travel clothes—tennis shoes, a sweatshirt, and sweat pants with my hair in a sloppy ponytail. I had planned to go straight to my room and freshen up before introducing myself to the conference hosts, but when I entered the hotel I walked right into the registration table.

"May I help you?" a woman asked in a tone that was really saying, I don't want to help you—please go away.

"Ah, yes . . . I'm Dr. Lorena Gonzalez, your speaker tomorrow," I said. I seldom mention my academic credentials but felt it was needed, given my "no-one-will-see-me" outfit. The woman behind the table looked confused. I'm sure my appearance didn't match her expectation of the event's key speaker. She immediately called out to her boss, and with some hesitation, she gave me the conference packet.

After that initial "welcome," I was a little worried. I'm not accustomed to getting such a cold reception, and I wondered if the message I had to offer would be well received. I kept hearing the words of my father: "*Nunca tengas miedo, siempre con orgullo de quien eres y de donde vienes*"/"Never fear. Always be filled with pride for who you are and where you come from."

He was right. I felt proud of being a daughter of immigrant/migrant parents who, with no more than a third-grade education, came to this country, left all their family behind, to pursue a dream. "*Siempre encomindate a Dios*"/"Always put yourself in God's hands," he said. "*Así lo hice yo*"/"That's how I did it."

My father did put his life in God's hands. He came to this country without understanding its ways and could only speak four words in English: I can do it! These were the words he used when he was asked to pick spinach, wash dishes, and cook pancakes. And as each day went by and he witnessed the life he could have in the United States, he worked harder and harder. He adapted to this new American culture but never compromised his beliefs.

The morning of the conference I arrived early at the room where I was to conduct my workshop and found a group of participants already meeting. I told them we wouldn't be starting for another hour. "Well, we have the room first, so if you don't mind . . ." one woman said as her voice trailed off. I left the room somewhat rattled, found a place to eat breakfast, and went back an hour later. A small group of about forty people had gathered by the time I got to the room. They all sat at the back four tables, leaving the tables in the front of the room vacant. While that workshop felt like the longest four-hour session I have ever conducted, the participants finally warmed up, seemed receptive, and were somewhat engaged.

At the end of the session, I collected my training materials and moved to the main ballroom where I was scheduled to speak. I wasn't sure where to sit, so I awkwardly approached the not-so-friendly woman who had checked me in. She suggested I sit at the head table with elected officials, leaders of the community, and conference organizers, all of whom seemed to know each other. "And who are you?" the woman at the head table asked in what seemed like a condescending tone. Before I could respond, she reached over me to say hello to the state senator sitting on my opposite side. "Do you know who he is?" she asked. I politely turned to offer my hand and introduce myself when she interrupted again and began to tell me about the senator's entire career. I smiled and ate my soup.

The senator spoke first. He was running for a congressional seat, and his speech focused on his goals for his constituency. As he spoke, I was losing confidence in what I had planned to say. This was a different audience, one I was sure wouldn't care about my family journey.

When he finished, a woman stepped to the podium to introduce me. The organizers had requested my biography, which I had provided, but the woman disregarded any formality and after a short sentence or two said, "Here is Lorena to say a few words." She had dismissed my family name altogether!

I felt very unsettled, but remembering my father's words, "Don't forget who you are and where you come from," I stood before the audience and began to share the story of my culture and journey. Without apology, I told the large group about my parents, their sacrifice, their dreams, and successes. As my presentation progressed, I saw tears mixed with smiles as the audience seemed to relate some of their own journeys with mine. And as I ended, there was resounding applause, and a standing ovation from many. The woman who had dismissively introduced me, wrapped her arms around me, and holding back tears, said, "That was beautiful, Dr. Gonzalez." Many others echoed her praise.—*LGG*

In middle school, my best friend was Jackie T. At first glance, we were an odd pair. She was almost the opposite of me in every way. She was tall, strong, bold, loud, and African American. However, it wasn't long before we found that our personalities complemented one another, so much so that we were often referred to as "salt and pepper." We were confident in our friendship and were a team that couldn't be separated. Whatever the activity, we sought each other out to do it together.

One of the most vivid and unforgettable conversations I had with Jackie was when I invited her over for a sleepover. Although it was the first time an African American had slept at our house, everyone welcomed her. As is the case with most sleepovers, the most insightful times were when the lights went out and the conversations occurred. We chatted about various things and finally got to the subject of our race. It was in this trusted and safe relationship with Jackie T. that I gained the courage to admit that we (my Hispanic community) thought all African Americans looked alike. I braced myself for her response, thinking she might become angry or resentful. She could have decided right there and then to call home and abruptly end the sleepover. Instead, Jackie's response was one I would not have predicted. She laughed out loud and said African Americans thought all Mexicans looked alike. I was stunned at her response. We don't at all look alike, I thought—that's ridiculous! I was about to *proceed down the path of being offended until I realized I was just as guilty of offending Jackie as she was of offending me. The communities we came from had both made the same error. We had not looked beyond the obvious to recognize the unique characteristics of one another.*

I learned a lifelong lesson at that sleepover with Jackie T. Among our many races and cultures, we have a tremendous opportunity to learn from one another, each bringing complementary talents, perspectives, and abilities. We can celebrate and complement one another in these differences, just like salt and pepper.
—LTC

RESPETO MISUNDERSTOOD

In my work, I often have the opportunity to meet extraordinary families in a variety of settings. One particular project was with a school district in the western region of the United States. At the beginning of the school year, I conducted a session with more than sixty families who shared their values and aspirations. *"Quiero que mijo sea educado, la educación es muy importante"*/"I want my son/daughter to be educated. Education is very important." *"Si es importante, los valores"*/"Values are important," one father said. *"Aqui en mi casa, se hace lo que mando yo"*/"Here in my house, they do as I say," he added.

I separated the parents and children and asked them to list their most important values. With only a few exceptions, the list for both groups was the same—respect, education, faith, family, and hard work. However, as one young woman explained how she applied these values, it seemed that there were more differences between the parents and their children than we first assumed. *"Yo tengo ideas y suenos pero por respeto a mis padres mejor me cayo"*/"I have ideas and dreams, but out of respect I have stayed quiet. I want to go to college and find a good job." Her parents listened intently as she continued, *"Me ofrecen una beca para estudiar en otro estado, pero no la aceptaré"*/"I've been offered a full scholarship to study in another state, but I will not be accepting." Her father responded, *"Pues si, se imagina ir sin protección de sus padres. Las niñas de este país se mandan solas"*/"Of course, can you imagine leaving home without protection from her parents. The girls in this country rule themselves." I asked the father to tell the group what he feared about letting his daughter go away to college. He explained that he thought she was too young and that, as a woman, she would not be able to defend herself. He believed she needed his protection.

I asked him to tell me why he loved his daughter. He said he loved her for being smart, astute, and hardworking, just like her mother. As he spoke about these two most important women in his life, he began to show a tender side to his tough, protective demeanor. He said when his wife of twenty years came to the United States, she didn't speak English and had no formal education. *"Me imagino que ella conocia este país muy bien"*/"I imagine she knew this country well?" I facetiously asked. As he began to respond with a "No," I knew by his expression that he was beginning to realize what I was getting at—his wife came to the United States without knowing the language or the area, and without the protection of her father. And now he was preventing his daughter from pursuing her dream for fear of the same challenges his wife had already overcome. In tears, he told his daughter she was like her mother, pursuing a better future. If his wife had the opportunity to pursue her dream, he needed to allow his daughter to pursue her dream as well.

In response to her father, the young girl expressed how grateful she was for all he had given her and would forever respect him and the family. I looked around the class, and every man, woman, and child was in tears. That day all of us grew in our understanding of mutual respect and shared dreams.

The young woman did leave home and thrived in college. Her parents began helping me lead workshops, speaking about the importance of holding true to one's own values while considering and adopting new ways of thinking. They became parent leaders in the community and mentored many newly arriving families.—*LGG*

As parents, our desire to protect and provide for our children can sometimes be a detriment to their growth and development. All one has to do is search the Internet on the keywords "helicopter mom" to know that overly protecting our children is not an issue exclusive to the Hispanic community. As parents, we

immediately want to keep our children close and sheltered. Some parents, particularly those who have experienced injustice and violence, want to make sure their children are not subject to the same difficulties they experienced. Like the concerned father, it is those difficult experiences that make parents the strong, resilient individuals they are. As parents, we must always be cautious and vigilant, but we have to give our children the freedom to pursue their God-given potential.—LTC

NADA SE LE COMPLICA

On my birthday in 2011, I sat with my friend and colleague, Lisa Treviño Cummins, president of Urban Strategies. Over lunch, we shared our dreams, as we often do, about the next year's goals, opportunities, and challenges. I mentioned to her my longtime desire to write a book combining many of the stories I have treasured over the years—personal stories that have made me who I am, and stories that have been passed along to me over the years. Her eyes lit up. "That's a fantastic idea. Do it," she said.

Now, if you know Lisa, you also know one of her favorite slogans is "Just do it," my version of *"Nada se le complica."* In other words, everything is possible and don't let anything get in the way. This belief is shared by my family, and many parents and children who come to this country to make a better life; *Nada se les complica.* I have had many wonderful mentors who equally encouraged me and pushed me to write a book, but Lisa was willing to support this venture by investing time and financial resources. This effort suddenly seemed very real and, honestly, very scary.

Knowing that my schedule would open up in mid-December from an intense season of travel, I mentioned to Lisa how the slower schedule might make it possible for me to start jotting some notes for a book project. I barely finished my sentence when she said, "That's a good idea. I will schedule a call with our editor tomorrow at 8:00 a.m." And shortly thereafter, as is her practice, when Lisa starts a task, she puts together a timeline, usually in my least favorite format—an Excel spreadsheet. Ugh! She suggested the holidays as a great time to start writing. I was spinning from her statement. I hadn't intended to jump into this tomorrow. But I remembered, *"Nada se le complica."*

Somehow the New Year seemed a better time to start; actually, anytime seemed better than tomorrow! My hesitation wasn't that I didn't want to write; it was fear of doing something entirely new. I rely on *el habla*/the spoken word. How could I write? I remembered the words of another mentor, Consuelo Castillo Kickbusch, who often talked about "little demons." She'd say, "They try to convince us we are not worthy or capable." I heard those little demons that day. I was scared! Who did I think I was? How could I write a book? But Consuelo would also tell me that those demons *"no valen"*/"are worthless." So with her *consejo*/advice in mind, I tried to ignore those demons and focus on the many gifts God had provided.

Our first call with the editor took place early the next morning. What is the book about? she asked. Who is the target audience? What is the purpose? These were questions I couldn't answer. We brainstormed and reviewed, set goals, and then our editor said those dreaded words, "Start writing."

This was a moment I had dreamed of for many years. But I couldn't start. I couldn't even type the first word. It was like being a new baby, excited to take off and explore its surroundings, but without stability to walk, much less run. After several false starts, I finally began to write my first story with self-doubt lingering just below the surface. When I finished, I was sure this project wouldn't work. But I continued, mainly because I felt all these stories I had in my heart needed to be shared with others.

Lisa was encouraging and kind, and most of all, she became a champion against the little demons that filled my head. She has offered a sisterhood I have never felt before. "I know how much this means to you," she told me one evening. "I want to help make your dream come true." I sat in silence. Did my *boss* just say she wanted to help me make my dream come true?

Lisa is an extraordinary leader. She sees far beyond her own gains and considers the dreams and goals of others. She is more than a boss. She is a partner in the struggles of the poor, a woman committed to family, faith, and community, a woman leaving a mark on this world, and a dream maker for me and many others every day.

I now remind myself that each one of us has the capacity to make dreams come true by offering words of encouragement to strengthen others, illuminating a path for someone who is lost and struggling, or listening to bring clarity to the visions and dreams of others. *"Nada se le complica."*—*LGG*

I am honored that Lorena shared this story, but the truth is, I inherited from my parents, and their parents before them, the attitude, perspective, and determination required to give life to the words "Nada se le complica."

Early in my career, I was focused on developing new programs and initiatives in an industry that at the time wasn't keen on innovation. My superiors would tell me—and I often internally repeated—"Find a way or make one." This was very empowering to me. And then, there were the beliefs I inherited as a child, tested as a young adult, and have since owned as my own: God is for me. Nothing is impossible if I am walking in His will. Nothing can separate me from His love. He will never abandon me. I can do all things through Him. This doesn't mean I don't have challenges and that I don't fail. I do. But I can be confident in know-ing that failure and challenges can be used for good and that I don't have to be afraid of taking risks or making tough decisions. Nada se me complica.——*LTC*

HONORING EL TRABAJADOR

Pop is the hardest-working man I know—and my whole family would agree. He worked difficult jobs in a variety of industries to ensure that he provided for his family. His example taught us that it doesn't matter what you do, it's that you do it with honor and excellence.

Pop's first job in this country was picking spinach. He then worked on the railroad, moved on to become a cook, and finally, spent thirty-two years as a welder at a company that manufactured trash trucks. He welded in temperatures over 100 degrees and wore several layers of clothing, gloves, and a face mask for protection from the burning welding sparks. Some days he would literally perspire his weight away.

Dad rang the doorbell every day when he came home from work. His hands were filled with his lunchbox and tools, and it was his way of announcing he had returned from a long day's work. My mother would run to greet him as he stood lifeless at the door, exhaustion imprinted on his face. Mom would take his lunchbox and tools and examine new burns on his forearms from sparks that seared through his three layers of clothing. Dad would then drag himself into our dining room, plop down on a chair, and stare into space. Sometimes he had enough energy to shower before dinner; at other times, he needed food to just make it through the remainder of the day. At whatever time he ate, my mother's meals always brought him back to life so he could do it all over again the next morning—a bowl of *caldo de res, calabasa con pollo,* or some *carne guisada.*

As a young girl I didn't see that his investment in work was unique because most of the men in my family worked hard—I thought it was normal for everyone to come home exhausted. On any given day while driving around the neighborhood my father would proudly point out a vehicle and say, *"Mira, yo hice esa troca"*/"Look, I made that truck." We examined the truck from afar and were filled with pride, "Wow, Pop, *¿todita?"*/"All of it?" For a kid, these were enormous impressions that translated to bigger-than-life pride in my dad and his work. He would go on to explain the different pieces he welded together that left his mark on each truck.

After thirty-two years as a welder, my father's retirement approached. Our family decided we would celebrate his working career in the same way he pursued it—with honor and dignity. Knowing he wouldn't want us to go to any trouble, we devised a plan we felt would honor him and involve some of his co-workers and employer. We considered doing our usual family party (bringing all 350 of us together!) but then decided to do something a bit more intimate. We wanted to make this a special celebration of Pop's lifelong commitment to working for our family and to give him the honor that employers often fail to give their blue collar workers, *los trabajadores.*

With great excitement, we put the details into place. We had to do this secretly, as Pop never wanted to attract attention, saying, *"No se preocupen . . . No hay necesidad de hacer nada . . . No mas estar con ustedes es suficiente"*/"Don't worry . . . It isn't necessary to do anything . . . Being with you is enough." My brother recorded Dad's favorite music, including Vicente Fernandez, Rocio Durcal, and Los Tigeres del Norte. I arranged for confetti and balloons, and my husband, Rene, prepared an ice chest with Pop's favorite drinks. And for the biggest surprise, we rented a white stretch limousine that would pick my dad up on his last day of work.

That Friday, at 3:00 p.m. when his shift ended, my father walked out of the welding shop for the last time carrying his lunchbox and tools. He was shocked to find our family waiting for him next to the limo. He was completely overwhelmed. Pop's co-workers were equally stunned, and we overheard one say, *"Mi familia . . . ni en burro viene por mi"*/"Not even on a donkey would my family come to get me." As Pop and his co-workers joined us, we opened the ice chest and began our celebration in the parking lot. At the invitation of the plant manager, we moved the limousine and the party into the warehouse and blew the car horn as the workers clapped and cheered for Dad. His boss gave a few remarks and then said, "Homer, it's obvious you are loved. Congratulations!"

Indeed, he is loved. Although he was a bit uncomfortable with all the attention, Pop felt revered and admired. We left the plant and spent the next few hours in the limo being driven around the city drinking champagne, listening to music, and singing our hearts out to the best songs ever. Those moments with Dad, on his last day of work, are unforgettable.—*LGG*

While my banking career focused on low-income populations, I watched my colleagues set up and manage trusts for families who wanted to invest wisely and minimize tax liabilities so they could pass their resources on to the next generation. One of the concerns raised by investors was how these financial resources would affect the values and work ethic of those who inherited them. More often than not, the individuals who were bequeathing their resources earned them through very hard work, perseverance, and a great deal of sacrifice. It was difficult for them, but this experience formed their values and perspective. Their fear was that in inheriting these resources, their children would miss out on the opportunity to develop an ap-

preciation for hard work and the things money can't buy.

As we work hard to generate some financial benefit for our children's future, we must remember to teach them those priceless values that will allow them to persevere, thrive, and have an impact on their community. We all want our children to have a better life than our own, but the measure of a "better life" must be about more than what we can purchase on a credit card. Tough love parenting is very difficult, but we must do everything to ensure that the work ethic of Lorena's father, of my father, and of many of our parents is not lost. Instead, we have the opportunity to teach our children that we must do our work—whatever it is—to the best of our ability. We have been created to do nothing less!—LTC

Traditions

A *tradición,* or tradition, is a practice, belief, or object passed down from family to family. Our Latino culture has many traditions that can vary based on country of origin. In my Mexican culture, two important traditions are *posadas* and *tamaladas.*

Posada

As far back as I can remember, our Christmas traditions in Mexico included a scripted *posada* followed by praying the rosary and then dancing, singing, and finally a piñata. My grandmother, affectionately known to us as Mama Chula, insisted that we kneel as we prayed the rosary. Of course, as children, we complained bitterly about this, as did our elder uncles. But deep down inside we reveled in the practice, not because we were the best Catholics, but because we had a competition to see who could stay on his or her knees the longest during the forty-five-minute ritual.

The *posada* began by selecting a few family members to stand outside the door and ask for *posada,* which means lodging or shelter, for Mary, Joseph, and the soon-to-arrive baby Jesus. This group was generally made up of children who could withstand the cold. Inside, another group of family members refused the entry of Mary and Joseph. After some time, the group indoors allowed the young ones to enter the house.

Adding to this tradition was the selection of *padrinos,* or godparents of the baby Jesus. The couple selected was generally young and newly married. *Padrinos* were allowed to ask the baby Jesus for a blessing. Most often the blessing they requested was to have children of their own. And very frequently, *padrinos* revealed in the spring that their blessing had been granted when they announced their pregnancy. It's no wonder I wound up with more than sixty first cousins!

After a forty-five-minute prayer vigil, we would stand, getting our balance after our legs went numb from kneeling, and then the dancing and singing would begin. The kids would hit the piñata until it cracked and delivered nuts and fruit. We would often celebrate until three or four in the morning.

As I became a young mother, I continued this *posada* tradition with my children even when we could not return to Mexico. I've come to learn that this tradition is more than the fun, laughter, and the contest of staying still during a very long prayer. The *posada* is a practice that has brought our family close together and united us in faith. We've had some minor alterations to our tradition. We've added some candy to the piñata's mix of nuts and fruit. We also added some contemporary music to our traditional hymns. Today our children invite their friends to participate as guests, or *padrinos*. One dear family, the Benavides, has shared this tradition with us for twenty-seven years. My daughter and niece talk about the day they will host a *posada* when the time comes to pass on Mama Chula's tradition. I think they are both ready.

Holding on to traditions with today's hectic pace is difficult, but these traditions are a wonderful inheritance for our children that help them form connections to family as well as to culture. The *tamaladas* and *posadas* are just two traditions that in some shape or form I hope to pass along to my children.—*LGG*

Tamalada
In our Latino communities, a number of foods or dishes take on an important role. Beyond the ingredients, cooking time, and calories, they stir up memories of people, places, and experiences. At the risk of missing some variations among our different Latin American countries and regions, some examples are mofongo and abichuelas (Puerto Rico), arepas (Columbia), pupusas (El Salvador), and ropa vieja (Cuba).

Important in our Mexican culture are tamales. Just the mention of tamales causes my imagination to go to another place and time. Physically, I remember the earthy smell of the corn husks and pork immersed in spicy seasonings. Emotionally, tamales remind me of laughter and friendship.

When I was young, my church youth group would make tamales to sell as a fundraiser for a youth camp or other activity. We would spend the week taking tamale orders from friends, family, and neighbors, then on Friday night at about 9:30 we'd start organizing the assembly line. First came those assigned to soak the corn husks and prepare them for the masa spreaders, followed by the meat fillers, the tamale wrappers, and finally, the stackers who would put the little gems into a pot to be steamed.

As the process began, so did the laughter. We would tease the corn husk group for being too slow or too fast, and the masa spreaders were too stingy or didn't leave enough room for the meat. This teasing led to laughter, jokes, stories, and finally conversations from the heart that carried on deep into the night. There was never any doubt that the next morning we would sell all the tamales—we always did. But more importantly, we rekindled our sense of community.—LTC

LIVING FAITH

One of the greatest inheritances I have received from my family, and one that I hope to pass on to my children, is that of faith. I am definitely not a theologian—nor am I even close to one—but when I use the term *faith*, I'm referring to the choice I made to believe, accept, and live for the God of Abraham, Isaac, and Jacob, and also my grandparents.

In March 1909, my maternal great-grandparents, Severo and Maria del Refugio Menchaca, carried their family of four, including an eight-month-old infant, from Mexico across the Rio Grande to Texas. While this move was only 200 miles away from their home, they entered a new land that had promised a new way of life—a just and fair government and an opportunity to pursue dreams through hard work and self-determination.

About 1928 the Menchaca family heard the good news of God, and eventually all of them became ministers, committed to living out their faith through service to others. Over time, that eight-month-old infant became my maternal grandfather, Severiano M. Menchaca, a leader in his community. While in Bible school, or seminary, my grandfather met and married my grandmother, Velia Flores, and shortly thereafter, they became pastors of a church in San Angelo. Later they moved to pastor a church in Laredo, Texas. It was at this Laredo church where my father and mother met as young children and eventually married. My parents raised my brothers and me in the church but encouraged us to choose faith for ourselves.

From this faithful environment, I have many memories that I hope to pass on to my children. One memory is of my grandfather playing the trombone in the church band. He continued playing and even had a few "jam sessions" when he was in his early nineties. Up front and "on stage," my grandfather would be joined by my father playing the electric guitar, my uncles all playing in the brass section with my Aunt Licha playing the piano, Uncle Joe Cantú playing the organ, and Uncle Joe Salazar passionately singing a song about the love of God. I later would join in on the piano, and my cousins would add their instruments and voices to a sing-along.

Whether in Laredo, San Angelo, or Houston (where they retired in their eighties), my grandparents pastored primarily poor Mexican immigrants. They witnessed many stories of disappointment, difficulty, and sorrow. They comforted and counseled families who suffered as victims of violence, racism, and economic pressures. In spite of these challenges and difficulties, the Menchacas always shared the little they had and welcomed others into their home, never considering anyone to be a stranger. Grandpa's motto was *"No damos porque tenemos, pero tenemos por que damos"*/"We give, not because we have, but we have because we give."

In addition to helping others who were suffering, my grandparents endured their own tragedies. On two different occasions, their homes were destroyed by fire. Another time, their house was lost to a flood. Such loss would cause many to abandon hope and faith, but it was in these difficulties that my grandparents leaned on their faith to sustain them. On each occasion, my grandparents would lead their family and church to rebuild their homes, their community, and their faith. It is no surprise that toward the end of his life, when I asked my grandfather to share with me his favorite scripture, he said it was Isaiah 43:

Do not be afraid, for I have ransomed you.
I have called you by name; you are mine.
When you go through deep waters,
I will be with you.
When you go through rivers of difficulty,
you will not drown.
When you walk through the fire of oppression,
you will not be burned up;
the flames will not consume you.
For I am the LORD, your God . . .

I'll always remember my grandfather, standing hand in hand with my grandmother, ending his prayers with an *"Amen y Amen."* He stood on his toes for the first *"Amen,"* then settled on his heels for the second

"Amen," as if to end his prayer with a physical exclamation point. My grandparents lived a full, abundant life that became a testimony of God's faithfulness. They lived a life I hope to emulate. *Amen y Amen.*—— LTC

As members of the clergy, the Menchacas were not exempt from the difficulties of their generation, but perhaps because of their calling, they faced even greater challenges. In many ways they were in a "triple jeopardy" situation. They had the combined challenges of being Mexican in an environment that discriminated against them; they were Protestant Mexicans in a culture that was historically Catholic; and they served in times of economic difficulty among a people who were among the most economically challenged. The Menchacas not only survived this difficult and complicated environment, but they thrived. Without the aid of the many leadership books and seminars that we have today, they marshaled the courage and determination to be faithful in their calling to Christ.—LGG

JUMPING THE FENCE

It might be said that I have been successful—but not by society's measures. I have been blessed with a husband and children that inspire me, parents and a family who have guided me, and a community of professional, personal, and faith companions. My Pop's first English words, "I can do it," has been a mantra for making dreams come true for me and my family. However, the dream of a college education was not to be mine until later in life. Instead, I chose marriage and children first and then returned to college as an adult with the responsibilities of a family.

I received my bachelor's degree with two of my three children in attendance, and I hoped this would serve as an example for them both. The graduation ceremony was overwhelming. The commencement address was given by Dr. Gloria Rodriguez, president and founder of AVANCE, a nationally recognized organization providing services to low-income families. As she ended her speech, Dr. Rodriguez referred to the fence that separated the university campus from the low-income housing project behind it. Dr. Rodriguez encouraged all of us to "jump the fence." She said we needed to use our talents and education to serve the people on the other side of the fence, to help them discover their talents and give them the tools to succeed.

I continued with my academic journey as our third child came into our lives. My children grew up surrounded by academic preparation. We often did homework together, cheered or consoled each other in success or disappointment, and asked advice on difficult topics, especially getting help from my eldest son on statistics. Even my husband returned to college to complete a master's degree.

All of us have tried to "jump the fence" and use our education and abilities to serve others, honor our culture, and build community. My son Rene, whom we call Lil Reenie, is an electrical engineer for a large family-owned grocery chain, H-E-B. He leads teams of employees to meet record-breaking goals. Most often his teams are made up of people like his grandfather, who share similar journeys, struggles, and challenges. He endearingly refers to these employees as *"paisas,"* brothers from the homeland. His connection to Mexico and culture is strong and constant.

My second son, Evan, made academics his career and teaches second grade in an all-Latino public school. His life experiences and understanding of our culture, and the struggles and triumphs that many families face in this country, creates a connection with his students and their parents. Even in his first year, he was rated in the top 10 percent of all the teachers in his school because of his innovative strategies to help children learn.

Amanda, our youngest, is now a woman I could only dream of becoming. She was born to lead! Now in her final year of law school, I have watched in awe as she tirelessly keeps pushing along. I observe the same level of dedication, or *ganas,* that her grandparents exhibited coming to this country, never giving up. That attitude will sustain her future career.

What I admire most about my children is how they love each other. These three young people are mutual supporters, elevating each other when they are down, and joining in celebration at each other's triumphs. I hope they have witnessed this example in the loving relationship I have with my brother, Arnol. Along with his wife, Monica, and their children, Nicholas and Michael, we are committed to using our gifts to "jump the fence" and serve others in love. Although not a perfect family, we continue to believe in our Pop's mantra, *"I can do it."—LGG*

LA BENDICIÓN

As much as we looked forward to our long summer visits in Mexico, our time would eventually end and we would return home. When our departure was imminent, we began filling our days and nights with last-minute visits to family, shopping for goodies we could find only in Mexico, and stolen moments with those we would dearly miss.

The morning of our departure, family members ran to my grandma's house to say goodbye. The last few minutes before we departed, we literally had "church" on the outside curb. Our family would join hands and form a circle around us as my grandmother, Mama Chula, led us in prayer. Everyone was emotional as she prayed in quiet whispers and made the sign of the cross over us.

As a young girl, it was common to receive this *bendición*/blessing from our elders as we went out the door. I never thought much of this, but as I grew older

I was embarrassed when my friends saw my grandparents praying over me, afraid they would think of me as strange. Over the years, however, the *bendición* became very important and made me feel protected by God and my entire family.

When my grandmother passed away, my mother inherited the duty of giving the *bendición*. Even if it wasn't possible to get together in person, over the telephone I could hear the soft whisper of these prayers as my mother began praying over my children.

Last Christmas my cousins Gustavo, Ana, and their children came to visit from Mexico. The travel to and from Mexico has become very dangerous as violence is rampant in the cities and the roads between us. Before their departure, I noticed my cousins gathering in a room at the back of our house. I asked if they had left something behind. *"La bendición,"* they said, as they moved into a circle and waited for the blessing. I realized I had inherited the role of my grandmother and mother to lead this tradition of giving the *bendición*.
—*LGG*

For my family, la bendición *was very similar to Lorena's. As we ended our visits and/or embarked on a long trip, we would gather together holding hands, and my grandparents, usually my grandfather, would*

thank God for our visit and would ask for His protection as we traveled. Today, we don't form the same circle upon every departure, but each day as my children walk out the door I say, "God bless you." With these three words, I am releasing them into God's hands, asking Him to protect them and to give them the discernment and courage to make good choices.—LTC

Our Bendición

As the final chapter of this collection of stories, we want to offer *la bendición* for you, the reader. Our prayer is that you will live a life without regrets and be admired for living out the same courage, hard work, and diligence of our ancestors. We hope that you will give sacrificially and serve others with humility, and that you will know inexplicable peace and be satisfied. In this, we pray that you will lead your family and community to pursue and celebrate the best of your inheritance.—*LTC & LGG*

ACKNOWLEDGMENTS

Any project depends largely on the encouragement and guidance of many. Our efforts in reflecting and writing could not have flourished without a few significant people. My greatest appreciation goes to Lisa Treviño Cummins for always having an attitude that is full of possibilities . . . *"Nada se le complica."* I will forever be grateful for her supporting a project that gave life to stories I carried in my heart.—*LGG*

Over the years, there are only a couple of individuals whom I've encouraged to put their stories to paper because they deserved to be shared with a broader audience. Lorena has taken me up on that challenge, and I'm glad she did. It has been a delight to work with Lorena as my friend and colleague on this project, which comes from the heart. Even though we have different backgrounds and experiences, we found so much to share, as evidenced by the tears and laughter that often filled our talks in writing this book. We both could understand one another and felt understood. This book also gave me an opportunity to remember the family, friends, and experiences that have profoundly affected me—and reminded me once again that I have so much to be thankful for.—*LTC*

We appreciate the guidance and support of Christy Rosché, our editor and friend, who saw wonder and beauty in stories we thought were just "normal."
—*LTC & LGG*

LORENA GARZA GONZALEZ

Through her lifelong commitment to leadership and service, Dr. Lorena Gonzalez inspires individuals to recognize and magnify their strengths for the good of others. Lorena combines practical and theoretical experiences to provide training and technical assistance that teaches practitioners, educators, policymakers, and community leaders how to build successful programs driving positive change. She also is instrumental in creating partnerships that strengthen the power of underserved communities.

Lorena was recently inducted into the prestigious Hispanic Scholarship Fund's Hall of Fame, where she received the "Optimista" award for achieving success through persistence in the face of adversity. Although her father had only a third-grade education, Lorena credits her father's four words, "You can do it," for helping her complete three degrees as a young wife and mother.

Lorena received her PhD in Leadership Studies from Our Lady of the Lake University in San Antonio, Texas, and her MA in Bicultural Bilingual Studies from the University of Texas at San Antonio. She completed post-doctoral work at Harvard University's Government, Executive Education Program.

Lorena and her husband, Rene, have three children and reside in San Antonio, Texas.

LISA TREVIÑO CUMMINS

As a third-generation American of Mexican descent, Lisa Treviño Cummins traces the formation of her identity and world view to her family and faith. She began her professional career at Bank of America where she pioneered community development efforts, providing national leadership focused on building public and private partnerships with faith-based organizations.

In 2001, Lisa helped launch the White House Faith and Community-Based Initiative. During her two-year tenure, Lisa was instrumental in creating initiatives that welcomed small community and faith-based organizations, increased federal resource accountability, and encouraged the removal of barriers that prevent new entrants into the federal funding stream.

Since 2003, Lisa has led Urban Strategies in its mission to tool, connect, and resource community and faith-based organizations committed to community transformation among the most vulnerable in our country.

Lisa earned her BS in Accounting from Trinity University in San Antonio and her MBA from University of Texas in San Antonio.

Lisa, her husband, and their three children reside in the Washington, D.C. area.

PHOTO ALBUM

Left to Right: Horacia M. Menchaca; Severiano M. Menchaca, age 9, 1907-2007; Nicanor M. Menchaca; Severo Menchaca; Maria de Refugio "Cuquita" Menchaca (Menchaca); Consuelo Menchaca (Antillon), 1901-1933; Cleofas Menchaca (Gonzalez).

Severiano M. Menchaca and Velia Flores (Menchaca)

Back Row Left to Right: Severiano M. Menchaca; Unknown; Horacio M. Menchaca; Unknown; Nicanor M. Menchaca. Front Row Left to Right: Unknown; Unknown; Cleofitas Menchaca (Gonzalez); Josefina Menchaca (Mendez).

Lorena Garza Gonzalez as a young girl with her father, Homer Garza, and mother, Maria "Choco" Garza.

Background Left to Right: Homer Garza, Maria Garza. Foreground Left to Right: Nancy Resendez, Edward Rene Resendez Jr., Iliana Aurora Resendez, Edward Rene Resendez.

CPSIA information can be obtained at www.ICGtesting.com
Printed in the USA
LVOW08s1231200816

501175LV00001B/39/P

DEC 23 2016

9 780615 668772